WHAT OBJECTS MEAN

Second Edition

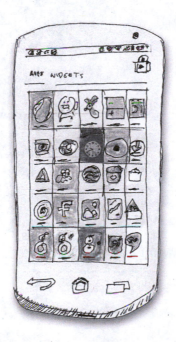

This book is dedicated to Wendy and Ivan Levison

WHAT OBJECTS MEAN

An Introduction to Material Culture

Second Edition

Arthur Asa Berger

Routledge
Taylor & Francis Group

LONDON AND NEW YORK

First published 2014 by Left Coast Press, Inc.

Published 2016 by Routledge
2 Park Square, Milton Park, Abingdon, Oxon OX14 4RN
711 Third Avenue, New York, NY 10017, USA

Routledge is an imprint of the Taylor & Francis Group, an informa business

Notice:
Product or corporate names may be trademarks or registered trademarks, and are used only for identification and explanation without intent to infringe.

Library of Congress Cataloging-in-Publication Data:
Berger, Arthur Asa, 1933-
  What objects mean : an introduction to material culture / Arthur Asa Berger. – Second edition.
    pages cm
  Summary: "Arthur Asa Berger, author of an array of texts in communication, popular culture, and social theory, is back with the second edition of his popular, user-friendly guide for students who want to understand the social meanings of objects. In this broadly interdisciplinary text, Berger takes the reader through half a dozen theoretical models that are commonly used to analyze objects. He then describes and analyzes eleven objects, many of them new to this edition—including smartphones, Facebook, hair dye, and the American flag—showing how they demonstrate concepts like globalization, identity, and nationalism. The book includes a series of exercises that allow students to analyse objects in their own environment. Brief and inexpensive, this introductory guide will be used in courses ranging from anthropology to art history, pop culture to psychology"—Provided by publisher.
  Includes bibliographical references and index.
  ISBN 978-1-61132-904-9 (paperback) — ISBN 978-1-61132-906-3 (consumer eBook)

  1. Material culture. 2. Material culture—Philosophy. 3. Culture—Semiotic models. I. Title.
  GN406.B473 2014
  306.4'6—dc23
                    2014007949

ISBN 978-1-61132-904-9 paperback

Contents

Preface

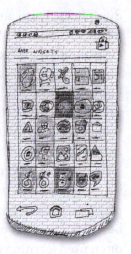

This book briefly explains six methodologies that you, the student, can use in various permutations and combinations to analyze material culture. These methodologies are:

Freudian Psychoanalytic Theory
Semiotic Theory
Sociological Theory
Marxist Theory
Cultural Theory
Archaeological Theory

I offer these theories because I believe the best way to make sense of objects and artifacts is to use relevant ideas and concepts from all of the theories in making your analyses—that is, for you to use a multidisciplinary approach to material culture.

After explaining these theories in Part I, in Part II I offer interpretations of a number of objects, based on the theories I've explicated and using material from authors in various

What Objects Mean, Second Edition by Arthur Asa Berger,
9–12. © 2014 Taylor & Francis. All rights reserved.

disciplines. I also apply a number of the concepts and theories found in the theory part of the book to these artifacts. I conclude each discussion of an artifact by offering some questions that will help you know what to look for as you analyze that and other artifacts. This book will help you learn how to make your own analyses and interpretations of objects and artifacts using combinations of semiotic, sociological, psychoanalytic, anthropological, economic (Marxist), and archaeological theories.

In Part III I offer some games that ask you to apply what you've learned in the first two parts of the book. These learning games can be played in class in groups of three students (which I've found to be the best arrangement) or can be assigned as homework. When I taught, I often used learning games in my courses and found that my students enjoyed them. At the same time, they learned a good deal from playing these games, because they were required to apply ideas and concepts they had learned.

The games can also be assigned as homework projects. That is, each student would be asked to play the game and come up with answers or whatever else was required. When I played the games in class, I selected one person as the "scribe," whose duty was not only to participate in playing the game but also to record the answers the group decided upon. After we'd devoted 20 or 30 minutes to the game, the scribes would report their team's answers to the class, and the whole class would then discuss the validity of the answers given by the various teams.

I believe that the best way for you to learn about material culture is for me to provide you with methodologies or techniques that you can use to make your own analyses of artifacts and objects of interest. Quite likely, you've already spent a good deal of time thinking about various objects and other kinds of material culture (things you wanted to buy and things given to you), but you've probably never been exposed to methods that will help you understand how to make sense of the objects and artifacts that play such a big part in your and everyone else's lives.

I have selected those aspects of the theories I deal with that are most useful in analyzing material culture and have not attempted a comprehensive look at any of the disciplines. I think using a number of disciplines will provide you, my readers, with a broader perspective on material culture than single disciplinary approaches. As you will see, material culture is a subject of interest to people in many different disciplines in the social sciences and humanities. In this second edition of *What Objects Mean: An Introduction to Material Culture* you will find the following enhancements:

Martin Grotjahn on symbols

A new definition of the concept of culture

Clifford Geertz on symbols

Roland Barthes on the semiotics of objects

Jean Baudrillard on the system of objects

John Berger on advertising and objects

Erik Erikson's psychoanalytic theories applied to smartphones

Marcel Danesi on myth and culture

My explanation of the myth model applied to objects

A new learning game based on the myth model

New chapters on Blonde Hair Dye, Bagels, Manga, and the American Flag

An updated chapter on technology and smartphones, sociability, and Facebook

I hope you will find this new edition both interesting and useful, and that it will help you see the objects around you and the objects you own in new ways.

Acknowledgments

I want to thank Mitch Allen, whom I've worked with since 1982, for suggesting I write this book and write a second edition of it five years later. We had lunch at a Dim Sum restaurant in San Francisco a number of years ago, and he thought it would be interesting for me to do more work on material culture. I had already written a book, *Bloom's Morning*, that analyzed various artifacts and rituals in a typical American's morning, so I was interested in trying my hand at the subject again. Originally, I was to write a book on methods and another one analyzing a large number of objects, but we finally decided it made more sense to put the two projects together into one book.

I want to thank my editor for the second edition, Ryan Harris, for his support and Ariadne Prater for her photos. In addition, I owe a debt of gratitude to all those who have written about material culture, from whose work I've greatly benefited. Thanks, also, to Michael Jennings, my copy editor; Hannah Jennings, my book designer; and to everyone else connected with publishing this book.

Part I
Theoretical Approaches to Material Culture

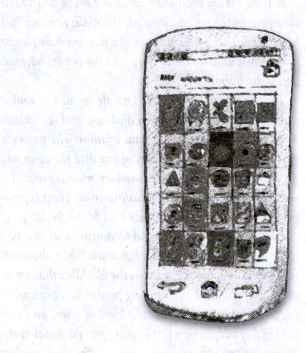

The objects which surround us do not simply have utilitarian aspects; rather, they serve as a kind of mirror which reflects our own image. Objects which surround us permit us to discover more and more aspects of ourselves. Owning a boat, for example, for a person who did not own a boat before, produces new understandings of aspects of his own personality; and also a new bond of communication is established with all boat owners. At the same time some of the power strivings of the individual come out more clearly into the open, in the speed attained, the ability to manipulate the boat; and the conquest of a new medium, water, in the form of lakes and rivers and the ocean, becomes a new discovery.

In a sense, therefore, the knowledge of the soul of things is possibly a very direct and new and revolutionary way of discovering the soul of man. The power of various types of objects to bring out into the open new aspects of the personality of modern man is great. The more intimate knowledge of as many different types of products a man has, the richer his life will be....

The things which surround us motivate us to a very large extent in our everyday behavior. They also motivate us as the goals of our life—the Cadillac that we are dreaming about, the swimming pool that we are working for, the kind of clothes, the kind of trips, and even the kind of people we want to meet from a social-status viewpoint are influencing factors. In the final analysis objects motivate our life probably at least as much as the Oedipus complex or childhood experiences do.

Ernest Dichter, *The Strategy of Desire*

1.

Making Sense of Material Culture

Every day we swim in a sea of images and navigate our way through a world of things, and many of the images we look at are of the things we have, want to have, or believe (thanks to advertising) that we need to have. Everyone has certain basic needs, such as housing, clothing, and food, but most people want many other things: automobiles, tools, accessories to our clothing, television sets, food products, computers, tablets, smartphones... the list goes on, almost endlessly. From our childhood until our old age, we are given things or continually buying things that we hope will make us healthier and more attractive, will show our love to someone—our partners, our children, our parents—and will enrich our lives and

What Objects Mean, Second Edition by Arthur Asa Berger, 14–28. © 2014 Taylor & Francis. All rights reserved.

those of our loved ones. What Dichter points out in the quotation that begins this chapter is that the objects we own also reveal a great deal about ourselves, and that studying objects is a useful way to find out about people and gain insights into, as he puts it, "the soul of man."

Defining Material Culture

The things we buy or are given are known as "objects" and "artifacts" in scholarly discourse, and these objects and artifacts form what social scientists call material culture. Material culture is the world of things that people make and things that we purchase or possess, so it is part of our consumer culture. Material culture is a subject of great interest to archaeologists, anthropologists, and many other kinds of social scientists and scholars because these objects provide information about what we are like and how we live now—and how we lived in earlier times. Some scholars use the term "object" for more or less contemporary material culture and "artifact" for the material culture of earlier times, but like many scholars of material culture, I see them as interchangeable.

In his book, *Objects: Reluctant Witnesses to the Past,* Chris Caple defines objects and artifacts (2006:1):

> The word "artefact" is derived from the Latin terms *ars* or *artis,* meaning skill in joining, and *factum* meaning deed, also *facere* meaning to make or do…. Thus an *artefact* can be considered to mean any physical entity that is formed by human beings from a nail to the building it is in. The term "object" is also widely used to refer to any physical entity created by human beings…. For the purpose of this book, the terms "artefact" and "object" can be used interchangeably.

Caple uses the British spelling for "artefact." For our purposes, I will define artifacts as *relatively simple objects showing human work-manship.* Automobiles and airplanes may have materiality, but they are very complex and complicated machines and, in fact, have many different smaller and less complex artifacts in them. Scholars may argue about definitions of material culture. Generally speaking, we can say that if you can photograph it and it isn't too large and complicated, we can consider it to be an example of material culture.

Material culture, we must recognize, is a kind of culture—a term that has hundreds of definitions. One definition of culture I like, because it shows the relationship between culture and artifacts, is by Henry Pratt Fairchild and is found in his *Dictionary of Sociology and Related Sciences* (1966:80):

> A collective name for all the behavior patterns socially acquired and transmitted by means of symbols, hence a name for all the distinctive achievements of human groups, including not only such items as language, tool-making, industry, art, science, law, government, morals and religion but also the material instruments or artifacts in which cultural achievements are embodied and by which intellectual cultural features are given practical effect, such as buildings, tools, machines, communication devices, art objects, etc.

This definition is useful because Fairchild points out that culture is based on communication and argues that artifacts embody and concretize various cultural values and achievements. Culture is passed on from one generation to the next and is, to a great degree, symbolic in nature. Cultural values and beliefs take form or are manifested in artifacts and objects—that is, in material culture. What this suggests is that we can use artifacts to help us gain insights into the cultures that produced them, if we know how to interpret or "read" them. Material culture gives us a means of understanding better the societies and cultures that produced the objects and used them.

Frank Nuessel offers another, more up-to-date definition of the term culture:

> The world "culture" comes from the past participle *cultus* of the Latin verb *colere,* which means "to till." In its broadest sense, the term refers to recurrent patterns of human behavior and associated

artefacts that reflect the beliefs, customs, traditions, and values of a particular society or group of people. This behaviour includes oral and written symbols such as language (folk talks, proverbs) as well as other traditions including dress, religion, ritual (dance, music, and other culture-specific rites), and so forth. Artefacts may include the representational arts such as paintings, pottery, sculpture, written literature, architecture, and the tools necessary to create them—all of which are transmitted from one generation to another. (2013:207)

Nuessel's article appeared in a book edited by Marcel Danesi, *Encyclopedia of Media and Communication* (2013), and offers us an insight into where the term "culture" comes from and into the way it has been understood by social scientists. My focus in this book is on the way that objects (he calls them "artefacts") reflect beliefs, attitudes, and values found in various societies. Freud said that dreams were the key to the unconscious; I have chosen artifacts and objects as the keys to what we might describe as our collective psyches.

The Blue Carbuncle as a Model for the Study of Material Culture

Reading people is a voyeuristic form of game enjoyed by many individuals who look at people and, based on a number of different matters, including their clothing, artifacts they may have (rings, earrings, canes, handbags, briefcases), facial expressions, and body language, try to figure out what they are like. Certainly, one of the greatest people readers was Sherlock Holmes, who was able to discern all kinds of interesting information about individuals who caught his attention for one reason or another. That is one of the reasons the Sherlock Holmes stories are so popular. After meeting someone and scrutinizing him or her carefully, Holmes is able to give detailed information about that person, based in large part on clues offered by the objects he or she wears and other clues to his or her activities and identities.

In *The Blue Carbuncle*, Holmes gives a large, wax stained, old hat that has come into his possession to his friend Watson and asks him what the hat reveals. Watson describes the hat as follows:

> It was a very ordinary black hat of the usual round shape, hard, and much the worse for wear. The lining had been of red silk, but was a good deal discoloured. There was no makers name; but as Holmes had remarked, the initials "H. B." were scrawled upon one side. It was pierced in the brim for a hat-securer, but the elastic was missing. For the rest, it was cracked, exceedingly dusty, and spotted in several places, although there seemed to have been some attempt to hide the discoloured patches by smearing them with ink. (Doyle, 1975:159–160)

Holmes says to Watson, "You know my methods. What can you gather about the individuality of the man who has worn this article?" Watson examines the hat and finds little of interest. "I see nothing," he says. Then Holmes replies:

> On the contrary, Watson, you can see everything. You fail, however, to reason from what you see. You are too timid in drawing inferences. He picked up the hat and gazed at it in the peculiar introspective fashion which was characteristic of him. "It is perhaps less suggestive than it might have been and yet there are a few inferences

which are very distinct, and a few others which represent at least a strong balance of probability. That the man was highly intellectual is of course obvious on the face of it, and also that he was fairly well-to-do within the last three years, although he has now fallen upon evil days. He had foresight, but has less now than formerly pointing to a moral retrogression, which, when taken with the decline in his fortunes, seems to indicate some evil influence, probably drink, at work upon him. This may account for the obvious fact that his wife has ceased to love him…He has however, retained some degree of self-respect. He is a man who leads a sedentary life, goes out little, is out of training entirely, is middle-aged, has grizzled hair, which he has cut within the last few days, and which he anoints with lime-cream. These are the more patent facts which are to be deduced from his hat. Also, by the way, that it is extremely improbable that he has gas laid on in his house. (Doyle,1975:160)

We can see how Holmes made his deductions about the individuality of the man who had owned the hat from the chart opposite. In essence, Holmes is offering an applied semiotic analysis of the hat.

Holmes's deductions strike us as ingenious, though the notion that a person with a large head must have a large brain in it and therefore a large intelligence is quite ridiculous. There are other deductions Holmes makes in the stories that are equally spurious. But this story, *The Blue Carbuncle*, provides an example that demonstrates what we do when we examine material culture. Watson is the typical person who cannot see very much in any objects because he doesn't know how to "read" them. Holmes is the scientific student of material culture who can use objects to determine a great deal about individuals who own and use them. Holmes can do this kind of analysis because of several things:

First, he has a great fund of knowledge about all kinds of things that he can use to interpret objects and other kinds of signs. Because he knows so much, he is able to make sense of many things that seem to be of a trivial nature. Second, he is very attentive to details and uses

Characteristics of Man (Clues)	Holmes's Reasoning behind Deductions
Man was intellectual	Cubic capacity of hat
Decline in fortune	Hat is three years old, of best quality but man hasn't been able to afford new one
Moral retrogression	Broken elastic not replaced
Foresight	Man had hat securer put on as precaution
Recent haircut	Hair ends, clean cut by a barber, stuck in lower end of hat lining
Uses lime-cream	Smell of hat lining
Goes out little	Dust on hat is brown house dust not gray street dust
Wife has stopped loving him	Hat hasn't been brushed for weeks
Out of training	Moisture in hat from perspiration, indicates man is out of shape
No gas in house	Wax stains from candles suggest he reads by candlelight, doesn't have gas

them to make inferences that will help him solve crimes. After Holmes explains how he has analyzed things, Watson replies something to the effect that what Holmes did was remarkable, to which Holmes says, "Elementary, my dear Watson." Readers take great pleasure in seeing how Holmes was able to make his deductions and inferences.

The more you know, the more information you have, and the more theories you have studied, the more you can see in things, so it is important to bring a store of relevant knowledge to objects when you are analyzing them. Any given object can be seen as a "figure" against the "ground" or "background" of the culture in which it was made and used. Objects also affect the cultures in which they are found, so analyzing them and interpreting their significance is a complicated matter.

The process of analyzing artifacts to find out about the cultures in which they were made works two ways: the objects tell you about the culture, and the culture tells you about the objects. When we deal with ancient cultures, we often know little about them and so use artifacts from earlier periods to make inferences and to try and figure out what life was like then. In contemporary societies, we use objects and artifacts to gain insights not provided by other methods of analysis.

On The Nature of Theory

We make sense of the world by fitting things that happen into theories we have that explain why they happen. Theories and concepts related to them help us understand various areas of life. One of the best

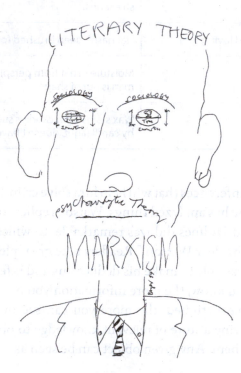

definitions of theories I know of is found in a chapter in *Media and Cultural Studies: Keyworks,* edited by Meenaskshi Gigi Durham and Douglas M. Kellner and titled "Adventures in Media and Cultural Studies: Introducing KeyWorks." The authors write (2001:3):

> A theory is a way of seeing, an optic, that focuses on a specific subject matter. The Greek word *theoria* signifies perspective and vision which centers upon specific topics, processes, and attributes, as a theory of the state focuses on how the government works. Theories are also modes of explanation and interpretation that construct connections and illuminate sociocultural practices and structures, thus helping to make sense of our everyday life, as an analysis of how Microsoft dominates the computer software field would indicate what particular issues are at stake. Thus, cultural and social theories are descriptive and interpretive; they highlight specific topics, make connections, contextualize, provide interpretations, and offer explanations. There is also a narrative component to theory as in Adam Smith's or Karl Marx's theories of capitalism which tell of the origin and genesis of the market economy, as well as describing how it works and in Marx's case offering a critique and proposals of revolutionary transformation.

Durham and Kellner point out that all theories are partial, so you always have to recognize their limitations.

To remedy the limitations that specific theories have, it is useful to use a number of different theories that enable you to gain different perspectives on whatever it is you are investigating. As Durham and Kellner explain (2001:4):

> Multiplying theories and methods at one's disposal helps to grasp the diverse dimensions of an object, to make more and better connections, and thus provide richer and more comprehensive understanding of cultural artifacts and practices under scrutiny.

This definition of theory is useful because it points out the limitations that specific theories have but also calls attention to the value of theories in helping us to interpret the significance of specific objects and to find relationships among phenomena that we might not have recognized without these theories.

What large theories do is generate smaller, less comprehensive theories and concepts that do the spade work in analyzing phenomena. For example, Freudian psychoanalytic theory is based on Freud's notion that our psyches have three levels: consciousness, pre-consciousness, and an unknowable unconscious, and three forces operating within our psyches: an id or desire, an ego or rationality, and a superego or conscience. As he writes in his essay, "Psychoanalysis" (1963:244):

> *The Corner-stones of Psychoanalytic Theory....* The assumption that there are unconscious mental processes, the recognition of the theory of resistance and repression, the appreciation of the importance of sexuality and of the Oedipus complex—these constitute the principal subject-matter of psychoanalysis and the foundations of its theory.

Within the larger framework of psychoanalytic theory, there are, then, other theories, such as the Oedipal theory, which argues that little children want to monopolize the attention of their parent of the opposite sex. And there are a number of concepts, such as Freud's defense mechanisms, that deal with repression, regression, ambivalence, and a number of other similar phenomena. These matters will be discussed in more detail in the chapter on psychoanalytic theory and material culture. So "large" theories generate smaller and more focused theories and concepts, and it is these theories and concepts we use when considering psychoanalytic theory to help us understand human behavior.

Let me offer an example of the relationship between behavior, concepts, and theories. We will take individuals who wash their hands two hundred times a day.

Behavior: Washes hands 200 times a day

Concept: Obsessive Compulsive Disorder

Theory: Psychoanalytic Theory

There are, of course, other psychoanalytic and non-Freudian psychoanalytic theories that deal with the human psyche, such as Jungian theory, so a psychology department in a university may have scholars with many different theoretical orientations—each of which has theories and concepts that adherents to these theories use to make sense of whatever it is they are interested in as far as the human psyche and human behavior are concerned.

Theories are like goggles that help determine the way we see the world, that point our attention to certain things, and that distract us from others. What Durham and Kellner argue is that the best approach to understanding cultural artifacts is a multi-disciplinary approach, since that approach enables us to see artifacts in all their many complexities. Single-disciplinary approaches are too narrow and often neglect important aspects of whatever it is that is being investigated.

Nietzsche and Perspectivism

In his book, *Will to Power,* the German philosopher Friedrich Nietzsche (1844–1900) adopts a perspectivist approach that involves recognizing the importance of different theories and methodologies to understand phenomena—a precursor of what we now call a multi-disciplinary approach to knowledge. He writes:

470. (1885–1886)
Profound aversion to reposing once and for all in any one total view of the world. Fascination of the opposing point of view: refusal to be deprived of the stimulus of the enigmatic.

481. (1883–1888)
Against positivism, which halts at phenomena—There are only *facts.*—I would say: No, facts is precisely what there is not, only

interpretations. We cannot establish any fact "in itself": perhaps it is folly to want to do such a thing.

"Everything is subjective," you say; but even this is interpretation invented and projected behind what there is.—Finally, is it necessary to posit an interpreter behind the interpretation? Even this is invention, hypothesis.

In so far as the word "knowledge" has any meaning, the world is knowable; but it is *interpretable* otherwise, it has no meaning behind it, but countless meanings.—"Perspectivism."

It is our needs that interpret the world; our drives and their For and Against. Every drive is a lust to rule; each one has its perspective that it would like to compel all the other drives to accept as a norm

(1885–1886)

No limit to the ways in which the world can be interpreted; every interpretation as symptom of growth or of decline.

Inertia needs unity (monism); plurality of interpretations a sign of strength. Not to desire to deprive the world of its disturbing and enigmatic character!

604. (1885–1886)

"Interpretation," the introduction of meaning—not "explanation" (in most cases a new interpretation over an old interpretation that has become incomprehensible, that is now itself only a sign). There are no facts, everything is in flux, incomprehensible, elusive; what is relatively most enduring is—our opinions. (1968)

Nietzsche's point is that interpretation is always an important part of any analyses we make. Take, for example, economics. Even when economists agree that certain statistics are accurate, they often disagree about how to interpret what these statistics mean. A Nietzschean approach means we look at love or life—or, in our case, material culture—not from "both sides now" but from all sides or, more accurately, multiple perspectives.

What fuels our battles over "truth" and "reality" and "facts" is, as Nietzsche puts it, "a kind of lust to rule." We want everyone else to accept our disciplinary perspective on things as the one and only true perspective. There is, we find, behind assertions philosophers and other kinds of scholars make about reality, a psychological need to triumph over or dominate others, or what Nietzsche described as a will to power.

The *Rashomon* Problem

Rashomon, directed by Akira Kurosawa, is a film that created a sensation when it appeared in 1951. When I saw it in 1951, it made a lasting impression on me, and I believe it has affected the way I conduct research and write books. The film, which takes place in the twelfth century, opens with a priest, a woodcutter, and another man in the Rashomon temple, seeking shelter from the rain. The woodcutter tells about his experiences observing what happened in a grove between a bandit, a samurai, and the samurai's wife.

Rashomon was based on two short stories by Ryunosuke Akutagawa (1892–1927), "Rashomon" and "In a Grove." The film is notable for its brilliant camera work and the superb editing and acting. It establishes

an important point—four people involved in an episode in a grove give four very different versions of what transpired. The film poses the question: Can we know reality? Is one of the stories true and the others fabrications? If so, who is telling the truth, and how do we find out who is being truthful? If we were to take *Rashomon* as an object of study, we would find that scholars from different disciplines would disagree about how to interpret it and who is telling the truth in the film. The Rashomon problem for us is this: What do we do when theorists from different disciplines disagree about how to interpret an artifact or object? What do we do when experts disagree?

We begin our study of theories useful for studying material culture with Freudian psychoanalytic theory, a controversial and fascinating exploration of the way the human mind functions. Freud's ideas have influenced thinkers in many different areas, and he is generally considered to be one of the most influential thinkers of the twentieth century.

The Middle Ages never forgot that all things would be absurd, if their meaning were exhausted in their function and their place in the phenomenal world, if by their essence they did not reach into a world beyond this. This idea of a deeper significance in ordinary things is familiar to us as well, independent of religious convictions: as an indefinite feeling which may be called up at any moment, by the sound of raindrops on the leaves or by the lamplight on the table. ... "When we see all things in God, and refer all things to Him, we read in common matters superior expressions of meaning."

William James, *Varieties of Religious Experience,*
p. 475

Here, then is the psychological foundation from which symbolism arises. In God nothing is empty of sense: nihil vacuum neque sine signo apud Deum, said Saint Irenaeus. So the conviction of a transcendental meaning in all things seeks to formulate itself. About the figure of the Divinity a majestic system of correlated figures crystallizes, which all have reference to Him, because all things derive their meaning from Him. The world unfolds itself like a vast whole of symbols, like a cathedral of ideas. It is the most richly rhythmical conception of the world, a polyphonous expression of eternal harmony. ...
From the causal point of view, symbolism appears as a sort of short-circuit of thought. Instead of looking for the relation between two things by following the hidden detours of their causal connections, thought makes a leap and discovers their relation, not in a connection of cause or effects, but in a connection of signification or finality.

Johan Huizinga, *The Waning of the Middle Ages,*
pp. 201–202

2.
A Freudian Psychoanalytic Approach

The basic premise of psychoanalytic theory, as Freud explained in his essay, "Psychoanalysis" (1922), is that *unconscious* mental processes exist and play an important role in our lives. As he explained (1963:230):

> Psychoanalysis is the name (1) of a procedure for the investigation of mental processes which are almost inaccessible any other way, (2) of a method (based upon that investigation) for the treatment of neurotic disorders and (3) of a collection of psychological information obtained along those lines which is gradually being accumulated into a new scientific discipline.

Freud saw psychoanalytic theory as an interpretative art, and this mode of

What Objects Mean, Second Edition by Arthur Asa Berger, 30–44. © 2014 Taylor & Francis. All rights reserved.

interpretation can be applied, as we shall see, to artifacts and objects as well as to psychological problems. As he wrote (1963:235–236):

> It was a triumph of the interpretative art of psychoanalysis when it succeeded in demonstrating that certain common mental acts of normal people, for which no one had hitherto attempted to put forward a psychological explanation, were to be regarded in the same light as the symptoms of neurotic: that is to say they had a *meaning*, which was unknown to the subject, but which could easily be discovered by analytic means.

Freud explained that we resist knowing the contents of our unconscious and repress recognizing the importance of the Oedipus complex and our sexuality. It is the hidden meanings and symbolic significance of various artifacts of material culture that a psychoanalytic approach to the subject attempts to discover. The quotation by Huizinga with which this chapter begins calls attention to the hidden meanings and unconscious significance of symbols and other aspects of life. There's more than meets the eye, he argues, to all things.

Artifacts and the Unconscious: Freud's Topographic Hypothesis

For Freud there are three levels to the human psyche: consciousness, pre-conscious (material we can access and of which we are dimly aware), and the unconscious, which we cannot access without guidance from psychoanalytic trained therapists. This is known as Freud's *topographic* hypothesis. It is useful to use the analogy of an iceberg to show how the three levels are related to one another. Consciousness, what we are aware of, is the part of the iceberg we see above the water. The preconscious is what we can dimly make out a few feet below the water line. And the unconscious is the inaccessible dark area that makes up most of our psyches, and that is buried deep beneath the water line. The important thing to recognize is that it is our unconscious, Freudian psychoanalytic theorists argue, that profoundly shapes our behavior.

We can suggest, then, that there are three levels that have to be understood when it comes to artifacts:

Consciousness: What an artifact does

Preconsciousness: Other aspects of the artifact's functionality of which we may be aware

Unconscious: Unrecognized symbolic meanings connected to the artifact

Presumably we are not conscious of the symbolic significance and importance of the artifacts we purchase or use. When we analyze an artifact, we should consider the meanings it has for different levels of our psyche.

Let's consider cigarette lighters, which have been studied by Ernest Dichter. Dichter, often described as the "father of motivation research," used depth psychology in interviews to discern how people felt about various products. What his research uncovered was that people often have attitudes towards objects of which they are unaware, attitudes that are hidden in the unconscious areas of their psyches.

For example, when his researchers asked people about cigarette lighters, they generally replied that they used them to light their cigarettes, so it was their functionality that seemed to be all-important. But

as his researchers probed further, they discovered that at a deeper level, subjects' cigarette lighters were connected to matters involving mastery and power and, specifically, the ability to summon fire at one's command. This is tied to mythological legends such as that of Prometheus and other myths involving fire. Finally, his researchers found that at the deepest level the feeling that one's lighter will work is connected to attitudes about sexual potency, and the flame of the lighter symbolizes, at the unconscious level, sexual union being consummated.

What follows is his analysis of their different levels of meaning.

Conscious: Light cigarettes

Preconscious: To summon fire

Subconscious: Sexual union ("Baby, won't you light my fire.")

We can use this theory about the levels of the human psyche to analyze other artifacts, to discover the hidden or unrecognized meaning that artifacts have for us.

A middle aged woman, whose legs were markedly bowed, changed the tables and chairs in her living-room three times before she could come to terms with her obsession about them. The first time, the tables and chairs had legs as bowed as her own. They were beautiful, costly pieces and everybody admired them, but they made her obscurely uncomfortable. She got rid of the lot and substituted others with delicate straight lines. These bothered her even more. Finally, after months of wracking indecision, she disposed of her problem by buying the kind of modern furniture which is all massive blocks and has no legs at all!

Another woman, preoccupied with her bowel movements, treated her whole house as though it were a gigantic bathroom. All the walls were bare and white and the curtains were made of some transparent plastic material. Decorative bowls, also white, and rather oddly shaped, rested on every available flat surface. A crowning touch, in which she took great pride, was a small fountain, set up in the wall which originally had held a fireplace.

Milton Sapirstein, *The Paradoxes of Everyday Life* (1955:98)

This insert shows the way unconscious processes work in people. Thus, the woman with bowed legs solved her problem by getting furniture with no legs, and the woman preoccupied with her bowel movements turned her house into a bathroom. In both of these cases, it was unconscious imperatives that shaped their behavior.

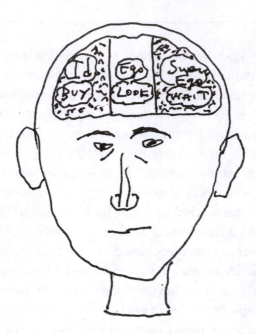

Id, Ego and Superego: Freud's Structural Hypothesis

Freud later suggested that there are three forces at work in our psyches, what is known as his *structural* hypothesis. This theory suggests that our psyches have three components: an id, an ego, and a superego. Charles Brenner, who wrote an influential book on psychoanalytic theory, described the structural hypothesis in his book, *An Elementary Textbook of Psychoanalysis* (1974:38):

> We may say that the id comprises the psychic representatives of the drives, the ego consists of those functions which have to do with the individual's relation to his environment, and the superego comprises the moral precepts of our minds as well as our ideal aspiration.

The drives, of course, we assume to be present from birth, but the same is certainly not true of interest in or control neither of the environment, on the one hand, nor of any moral sense or aspirations on the other. It is obvious that neither of the latter—that is, neither the ego nor the superego—develops till sometime after birth.

Psychoanalytic theory suggests that the ego performs a delicate balancing act between id forces (our drives, "I want it all now") and the superego forces (our sense of guilt, conscience, and similar phenomena). The id provides energy, but it is unfocused and dissociated. It has to be controlled to some degree since we must live in society. The superego provides restraint, but if too strong, it inhibits us too much, and we become overwhelmed by guilt. The ego stores up experiences in the memory by which it guides us and mediates between id and superego forces. People who have overly powerful ids or superegos that dominate the ego elements in their psyches generally have psychological problems and experience difficulties in their lives.

It is possible to classify artifacts according to whether they are connected primarily to id, ego, or superego elements in our psyches. What follows is my suggestion about how one might classify a number of different objects using Freud's typology.

Id	Ego	Superego
Barbie Doll	Dictionaries	Bible
Playboy Magazine	Textbooks	Book of Fables
Bottle of Liquor	Science Toys	Holy Water Vessel

I used the term "primarily" because Freud's topographic theory suggests that objects can have different levels of significance.

Psychoanalytic theory also suggests that the ego can also employ a number of defense mechanisms to help it control id and superego elements in our psyches, prevent anxiety and overwhelming guilt, and control our instincts. We are generally not conscious of our use of these defense mechanisms, and sometimes they are not successful in controlling our ids and superegos. Among these defense mechanisms are:

Ambivalence: a simultaneous feeling of attraction and repulsion

Avoidance: refusal to face matters that distress us

Denial: inability to accept reality of things that generate anxiety

Fixation: obsessive attachment to something, generally as result of trauma

Identification: desire to be like someone

Rationalization: offering excuses for untoward behavior

Regression: individuals return to an earlier stage of development

Repression: barring certain phenomena from consciousness

Suppression: putting certain things out of mind

When using psychoanalytic theory, we can consider these defense mechanisms in addition to the unconscious significance of artifacts and the relationship among these three elements of the psyche as we analyze objects of material culture.

For example, we may identify with some sports hero and purchase a brand of running shoe or watch advertised by that figure. We may develop a fixation about shoes and purchase many more pairs than we can possibly use. Imelda Marcos, the wife of Ferdinand Marcos, the former president of the Philippines, is famous (infamous may be more correct) for having purchased thousands of pairs of shoes, reflecting a fixation she had for them.

We may rationalize our purchase of some expensive perfume or body fragrance by convincing ourselves that it will have a positive impact on our social life. When we are adults and buy an ice cream cone, this can be considered a form of momentary regression in the service of our egos. Much of this works at the unconscious level, so we aren't aware that we are using defense mechanisms, such as rationalization, to justify our longing for, and purchasing of, artifacts of all kinds.

Symbolic Aspects of Material Culture

There is another important aspect of psychoanalytic theory as it relates to material culture that must be considered—namely, the importance of symbolism. As Hinsie and Campbell explain in their book, *Psychiatric Dictionary* (1970:734), we can understood symbolism as

> the act or process of representing an order or idea by a substitute object, sign, or signal. In psychiatry, symbolism is of particular importance since it can serve as a defense mechanism of the ego, as where unconscious (and forbidden) aggressive or sexual impulses come to expression through symbolic representation and thus are able to avoid censorship.

Symbols are, technically speaking, things that stand for other things. According to Hinsie and Campbell, we often disguise unconscious aggressive and sexual desires by using symbols, and doing so enables us to escape from the strictures of the superego.

Freud suggested that most of the symbolic phenomena in dreams have a masked sexual content, and this masking protects dreamers and prevents the superego from waking them. As Freud wrote in the tenth lecture of his *A General Introduction to Psychoanalysis* (1953:161):

> The penis is symbolized primarily by objects which resemble it in form, being long and upstanding, such as sticks, umbrellas, poles, trees and the like; also by objects which, like the thing symbolized, have the property of penetrating and consequently of injuring the body—that is to say pointed weapons of all sorts: *knives, daggers, lances, sabers;* fire-arms are also similarly used: *guns, pistols and revolvers.*

Freud is discussing symbols that are found in dreams, but it is also quite likely that many of these objects or phallic symbols have the same significance, though this significance is not recognized by us, in our everyday lives.

Freud also discussed how female genitalia were symbolized in dreams (1953:163–164):

The female genitalia are symbolically represented by all such objects as share with them the process of enclosing a space or are capable of acting as receptacles: such as *pits, hollows and caves,* and also *jars and bottles;* and *boxes of all sorts and sizes...Ships* too come into this category. Many symbols refer rather to the uterus than to the other genital organs: thus *cupboards, stoves* and above all *rooms...*The breasts must be included amongst the organs of sex; these, as well as the larger hemispheres of the female body, are represented by *apples, peaches and fruit in general.* The pubic hair in both sexes is indicated by *woods and thickets.*

Freud said that sexual intercourse was often represented in dreams by activities such as riding, dancing, sliding, gliding, and experiencing violence of some kind—all of which enable us to disguise our sexual desires and fulfill our unconscious wishes of a sexual nature.

It is reasonable to suggest that, since sex plays such an important role in our unconscious wishes, desires, and fantasies, and in our conscious activities, many artifacts incorporate, either consciously or

Male	Female
Sticks	Bottles
Umbrellas	Cupboards
Knives	Stoves (ovens)
Guns	Microwaves
Toothbrushes	Refrigerators
Pens	Dishwashing machines
Jackhammers	Pots

unconsciously, sexual symbols in their design. We can also classify objects according to whether they are symbolically male/phallic in nature or female/vaginal/utero in nature.

Psychoanalytic theory would suggest that people are not aware of the symbolic significance of the objects they use, but quite obviously a large number of artifacts have either a masculine penetrating or female incorporative character to them. We disguise the sexual nature of objects in our dreams so our dream censor or superego will not wake us, so disguising the sexual nature of objects is functional. Freud also has some interesting theories about how we develop sexually that can be used to analyze objects of interest to us.

It's worth considering what Clifford Geertz writes about symbols in *The Interpretation of Cultures* (2000:45):

> Thinking consists not of "happenings in the head" (though happenings there and elsewhere are necessary for it to occur) but of a traffic in what have been called, by G. H. Mead and others, significant symbols—words for the most part but also gestures, drawings, musical sounds, mechanical devices like clocks, or natural objects like jewels—anything, in fact, that is disengaged from its mere actuality and used to impose meaning upon experience. From the point of view of any particular individual, such symbols are largely given. He finds them already current in

the community in which is he is born and they remain, with some additions, subtractions, and partial alterations he may or may not have had a hand in, in circulation when he dies. While he lives he uses them, or some of them, sometimes deliberately and with care, most often spontaneously and with ease, but always with the same end in view: to put a construction upon the events through which he lives, to orient himself within "the ongoing course of experiencing things," to adopt a vivid phrase of John Dewey's.

Geertz points out that much of our thinking is based on "significant" symbols and that we use symbols to "impose meaning" on things; our understanding of symbols is connected to the communities in which we are born. He mentions that "mechanical devices"—what I describe as objects—play an important role in our thinking.

In his book, *The Voice of the Symbol,* Martin Grotjahn, a psychiatrist and psychoanalyst, writes that a symbol is a "message from our unconscious which communicates truth, beauty and goodness" (1971:xi). He adds:

> A book on the symbol is therefore a book about life and its mastery. It is also a book about death, which we must master in order to progress from maturity to wisdom. Insight into one's own unconscious or that of our fellow man is insight communicated by the symbol. Insight is inner vision and therefore closely related to art and intuition, to tact and empathy.

Symbols, Grotjahn explains, play an important role in our understanding of life and of art, and it was Freud who alerted us to the significance of symbols in our lives—in our dreams, our psyches, and our everyday activities (xii).

Sexual Development and Material Culture

Freud believed that individuals pass through a number of different stages in their sexual development as they grow older. These stages are described by Charles Brenner in *An Elementary Textbook of Psychoanalysis* (1974:24):

For the first year and a half of life, approximately, the mouth, lips and tongue are the chief sexual organs of the infant. By this we mean that its desires as well as its gratifications are primarily oral ones…In the next year and a half, the other end of the alimentary canal, that is the anus, comes to be the most important site of sexual tensions and gratifications… Toward the close of the third year of life the leading sexual role begins to be assumed by the genitals, and it is normally maintained by them thereafter. This phase of sexual development is referred to as the phallic one for two reasons. In the first place, the penis is the principal object of interest to the child of either sex. In the second, we believe the girl's organ of sexual excitement and pleasure during this period is her clitoris, which is embryonically the female analogue of the penis.

The last stage, which children reach upon puberty, when they learn to focus their attention on members of the opposite sex, is the genital stage.

According to Freud, young boys between approximately two and five develop an unconscious desire for their mothers and hostility towards their fathers—what he called the Oedipus Complex, after the Greek myth in which Oedipus, without recognizing what he was doing, killed his father and married his mother. Eventually this matter is resolved in boys by their developing anxiety about being castrated, what Freud called castration anxiety. Young girls also wish to supplant their mothers but resolve their problem in a different way, essentially by finding someone to supplant their father, namely a husband or lover.

We can use Freud's typology to classify objects according to whether they are primarily oral, anal, phallic, or genital in nature, recognizing that people who use these objects are generally not aware of their sexually symbolic nature.

Oral	Anal	Phallic	Genital
Pipe	Potty	Cigar	Condom
Pacifier	Enema	Video game joystick	Vibrator

Some objects may combine several different aspects, but usually it is possible to determine that one is basic. Thus, for example, a toothbrush is primarily phallic but used for oral purposes.

Conclusions

Psychoanalytic theory provides us with a large number of concepts that enable us to analyze material culture in terms of the way artifacts reflect various unconscious needs and desires and relate to our psychological makeup. We can use the ideas Freud and other psychoanalytic theorists have developed about the nature of the human psyche, about the importance of symbolic phenomena in dreams, about our use of defense mechanisms, and about the stages in our sexual development to gain insights into the reasons certain artifacts play such an important role in our lives as individuals and collectively in our societies.

French toys always mean something, and this something is always entirely socialized, constituted by the myths or techniques of modern adult life: the Army, Broadcasting, the Post Office, Medicine (miniature instrument-cases, operating theatres for dolls), School, Hair-Styling (driers for permanent waving), the Air Force (Parachutists), Transport (trains, Citroens, Vedettes, Vespas, petrol stations), Science (Martian toys).

The fact that French toys literally prefigure the world of adult functions obviously cannot but prepare the child to accept them all, by constituting for him, even before he can think about it, the alibi of a Nature which has at all times created soldiers, postmen and Vespas. Toys here reveal the list of all the things the adult does not find unusual: war, bureaucracy, ugliness, Martians, etc. It is not so much, in fact, the imitation which is the sign of an abdication, as its literalness: French toys are like a Jivaro head, in which one recognizes, shrunken to the size of an apple, the wrinkles and hair of an adult. There exist, for example, dolls which urinate; they have an oesophagus, one gives them a bottle, they wet their nappies; soon, no doubt, milk will turn to water in their stomachs. This is meant to prepare the little girl for the causality of house-keeping, to "condition" her to her future role as mother.

Roland Barthes, *Mythologies*

3.
Semiotic Approaches to Material Culture

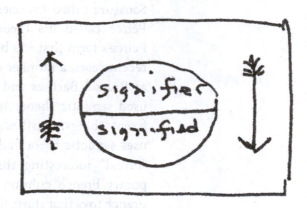

Semiotics (from the Greek term for signs, *sēmeîon*) is the science of signs, and a semiotic approach to material culture regards artifacts as signs whose meaning and significance have to be determined by the use of semiotic concepts. Signs are things that stand for other things or anything that can be made to stand for something. Think, for example, of the American flag. It is a sign that stands for the United States and for various values, historical events, and other matters connected to the country. Words are important kinds of signs. Thus the word "tree" stands for "a woody perennial plant having an elongated main stem." Artifacts are also signs.

There were two founding fathers of semiotics—the Swiss linguist Ferdinand de Saussure (1857–1913) and the American philosopher Charles Sanders Peirce (1839–1914).

What Objects Mean, Second Edition by Arthur Asa Berger, 46–60. © 2014 Taylor & Francis. All rights reserved.

Saussure called his science "semiology" and Peirce called his theory "semiotics." It is Peirce's term that has become dominant. In recent years, a number of semioticians, such as Roland Barthes and Umberto Eco, have used semiotic theory to analyze many different things. Barthes's book, *Mythologies,* uses semiotic theory and Marxist theory to "reveal" interesting things about contemporary French culture, as his discussion of French toys that starts this chapter suggests.

Saussure on Signs

Saussure set out the fundamentals of what he called semiology in his book, *Course in General Linguistics.* This book, primarily a collection of notes to his essays by his students Charles Bally and Albert Sechehaye at the University of Geneva, was published in 1915. It was translated into English by Wade Baskin and published in 1959 by The Philosophical Library and in 1966 by McGraw-Hill. In this book is found what might be thought of as the charter statement of semiotics (1966:16):

> Language is a system of signs that express ideas, and is therefore comparable to a system of writing, the alphabet of deaf-mutes, symbolic rites, polite formulas, military signals, etc. But it is the most important of all these systems.
>
> *A science that studies the life of signs within society* is conceivable; it would be a part of social psychology and consequently of general psychology; I shall call it *semiology*

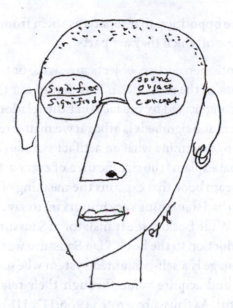

(from Greek *sēmeîon* "sign"). Semiology would show what constitutes signs, what laws govern them. Since the science does not yet exist, no one can say what it would be; but it has a right to existence, a place staked out in advance.

Semiotics studies signs in society, which means it is a social science, and explains what signs are and how they function. These matters are, it turns out, quite complicated.

Saussure offered a definition of a sign, which he explained was comprised of two parts—a sound-image and a concept (1966:66):

The linguistic sign united, not a thing and a name, but a concept and a sound-image. ... I call the combination of a sign and a sound-image a *sign,* but in current usage the term generally designates only a sound-image, a word, for example (*arbor,* etc.). ... Ambiguity would disappear if the three notions involved here were designated by three names, each suggesting and opposing the others. I propose to retain the word *sign* [*signe*] to designate the whole and to replace *concept* and *sound-image* respectively by *signified* [*signifié*] and *signifier* [*signifiant*]; the last two terms have the advantage of indicating the opposition that separates them from each other and from the whole of which they are parts.

From a semiotic perspective, objects are signs, or technically signifiers, and the task of the semiotician is to figure out their various signifieds. This is complicated by the fact that the relationship that exists between signifiers and signifieds is arbitrary, a matter of convention. So we always have to determine what an artifact signifies and cannot find a "rule book" that explains the significance of every artifact, just as we cannot find a dream book that explains the meaning of every dream.

Saussure also had something very important to say about the nature of concepts. As Wade Boskin, the translator of Saussure's book, points out in his introduction to the book, "De Saussure was among the first to see that language is a self-contained system whose interdependent parts function and acquire value through their relationship to the whole" (1966: xii). As Saussure wrote (1966:117, 118):

> It is understood that concepts are purely differential and defined not by their positive content but negatively by their relations with the other terms of the system. Their most precise characteristic is in being what the others are not…signs function, then, not through their intrinsic value but through their relative position

He summed up his ideas on this subject by writing "in language there are only oppositions" (1966:120), and these oppositions aren't between positive terms.

In essence, we find meaning in concepts (and other aspects of language and life) by setting up oppositions. So what this means is that—and this sounds like doubletalk—concepts derive their meaning from their opposites. Thus, happy is only meaningful as the opposite of sad, and healthy is only meaningful as the opposite of sick. It is the relationships that confer meaning on concepts and, by implication, artifacts and objects that are part of material culture. I should also point out that oppositions are not the same things as negations. The negation of happy is unhappy; the opposite of happy is sad. They are not the same thing.

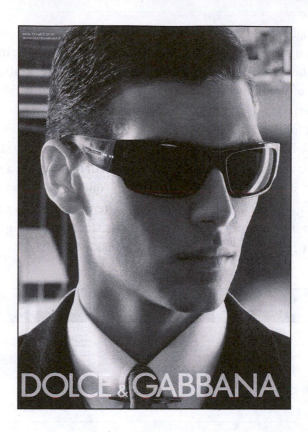

What Saussure called a "sound-image" becomes an object or signifier. The game is to discern what is signified by this object. In some cases, to complicate matters, an artifact can be thought of as a sign system, containing a number of different signifiers and signifieds. For example, a photograph of a person may contain many different signifiers: hats, eyeglasses, jewelry, shoes, attaché cases, briefcases, purses, canes, and so on.

We can also consider objects in terms of their size, shape, texture, color, and grain.

Problems with Interpreting Signs

We saw in the Sherlock Holmes discussion in the first chapter that an object, such as an old hat, can contain a number of different signifiers, so we might say that objects are to be thought of as signs and, in most cases, as sign systems—signs with many other signs contained within them. Thus, the hat that Sherlock Holmes gave to Watson can be thought of as a sign system full of smaller signifiers: the size of the hat, the material it was made of, and so on.

What follows is a list of artifacts or objects that function as signifiers, and what is left to be inferred by analysts is what they signify. The signifieds are all based on convention, and in many cases a number of different signifieds can be inferred from one signifier, which makes analyzing signifiers difficult at times. There are also the matters of conventions changing and of lying with signs—wearing signs that give false impressions, a matter to be discussed shortly.

Signifier/Object	Signified(S)
Bowler	Englishman
Bow tie	Intellectual
Cowboy hat	Cowboy, Westerner
Baseball hat worn backwards	Hip-Hop
Name brand eyeglasses	Stylish, fashionable
Analog watch	Old fashioned
Digital watch	Modern
Suspenders	Old fashioned
Black turtleneck sweater	Arty? Beatnik?
Expensive handbag	Style conscious, wealthy

We spend a good deal of effort in our everyday lives in observing signs and trying to interpret their meaning. When it comes to material culture, these signs involve body ornaments, clothes, shoes and other things—each of which, due to its styling, brand, cost and other factors, conveys different things. For example, there is the matter of whether an object is a "top of the line" smartphone like an iPhone or a cheaper brand of smartphone that might cost the same amount of money as an "entry level" version of the more expensive brand. So we have to consider the brand, the cost, whether an object is contemporary or old fashioned, whether it is the real thing or a "knock off," and so on. This means we have to have a certain amount of product knowledge and general knowledge in order to determine how to interpret an object from a semiotic perspective. We gain this product knowledge thanks to advertising and the media.

Peirce on Signs

Charles Sanders Peirce is the other found-ing father of modern semiotics and the person who gave the subject its name. He suggested that the universe is made up of signs and that the interpreters of signs have to supply some of the meanings, writing that a sign is "something which stands to somebody for something in some respect or capacity" (quoted in Zeman, 1977:24). Peirce elaborated a trichotomy, saying that

there are three kinds of signs: iconic signs that signify by resemblance; indexical signs that signify by cause and effect; and symbolic signs, whose meaning must be learned.

We can see these three aspects of signs in the chart below:

	Icons	Indexes	Symbols
Mode	Resemblance	Causal connection	Convention
Process	Can see	Can determine	Can learn
Examples	Statue of person	Bomb fragments	Crucifix, flags

We can combine Saussure's and Peirce's approaches to semiotics and use both approaches to analyze material culture. Thus, we can see objects in terms of whether they are iconic, indexical, or symbolic, and we can see them as signifiers that have signifieds to be discerned.

Photographs and other objects, such as coins, which often have images of important personages on them, are examples of iconic objects. Crucifixes and flags are symbolic in that their meaning has to be learned and are thus cultural in nature. Bomb fragments enable experts to determine what kind of explosive was used and in some cases where the explosive and bomb paraphernalia come from.

Jonathan Culler has explained the importance of semiotics as follows:

The notion that linguistics might be useful in studying other cultural phenomena is based on two fundamental insights: first, that social and cultural phenomena are not simply material objects or events but objects and events with meaning, and hence signs; and second, that they do not have essence but are defined by a network of relations. (1976:4)

Thus, a semiotic approach to material culture involves searching for the way these objects function as signs and generate meaning to others. From a semiotic perspective, nothing has meaning in itself; an object's meaning always derives from the network of relations in which it is embedded. Thus, when we think about a watch, we have to consider whether it is digital or analogue; entry-level, mid-level, or high end; and how it compares to other watches offered by other companies.

Roland Barthes on the Semiotics of Objects

In Roland Barthes's *The Semiotic Challenge* (1988), he has a chapter titled "Semantics of the Object," in which he offers some insights into the role of semiotics in analyzing material culture. He writes (168):

> It is in this general context of semiological inquiry that I should like to offer some rapid and summary reflexions on the way in which objects can signify in the contemporary world. And here I must specify at once that I am granting a very strong sense to the

word *signify;* we must not confuse signify with communicate: to *signify* means that objects carry not only information, in which case they would communicate, but also constitute structured systems of signs, i.e, essentially systems of differences, of oppositions and contrasts.

He points out that we conventionally define an object as "something used for something," and then adds (1988:169; italics in original), "There is virtually never an object *for nothing.*" There is a paradox, Barthes suggests, that involves objects (169–170):

> The paradox I want to point out is that these objects which always have, in principle, a function, a utility, a purpose, we believe we experience as pure instruments, whereas in reality they carry other things, they are also something else: they function as the vehicle of meaning. …There is always a meaning which overflows the object's use…there is no object which escapes meaning.

The problem in studying the meaning of objects, Barthes cautions, is what he describes as the obstacle of the obvious. We have to move beyond what is obvious and an examination of the object detached from its role in the world. We must look at the way objects are used in advertising, films, and the theater to gain a better understanding of what they mean for people.

Barthes wrote his article in 1964, well before he was to write his most well-known book, *Mythologies,* and in his article on objects we can see he was beginning to examine aspects of French culture that would lead to *Mythologies.* He ends the article by discussing the way people convert objects into what he calls "pseudo-nature," and that theme is to be of major importance in *Mythologies.*

On the Veracity of Signs

One of the problems with signs, that they can be used to lie, was pointed out by the distinguished semiotician Umberto Eco. As he wrote in his *A Theory of Semiotics* (1976:7):

Semiotics is concerned with everything that can be taken as a sign. A sign is everything which can be taken as significantly substituting for something else. This something else does not necessarily have to exist or to actually be somewhere at the moment in which a sign stands for it. Thus semiotics is in principle the discipline studying everything which can be used in order to lie. If something cannot be used to tell a lie, conversely it cannot be used to tell the truth; it cannot be used "to tell" at all. I think that the definition of a "theory of the lie" should be taken as a pretty comprehensive program for a general semiotics.

Eco cautions us to recognize that signs can be used to mislead others, so we must always approach objects with a note of caution.

We can see how people can use signs to "lie" in the chart that follows.

Objects	Means of Misleading
Elevator shoes	Short height is disguised
Wigs	Bald person covers up baldness
Imitation crab	Fake crab is much cheaper
Falsies	Large breasts
Clothes of opposite sex	Transvestism

It is obvious from this list that by using certain objects we can manipulate our identities and "lie" with signs. This process, lying with signs, is found not only in our objects but also in other aspects of our everyday life—including the design of objects, facial expressions, body language and language itself. A great deal of what we think of as "people watching" involves examining different kinds of material culture that people are wearing or using: hats, jewelry, clothes, shoes, handbags, briefcases, and so on. One problem we face in "people watching" is that we have no way of knowing, most of the time, whether people are lying with signs—some blondes are really brunettes, that beautiful blonde you see may really be a man, and that handsome man may be a woman.

Denotation and Connotation

In semiotic theory, denotation and connotation play an important role. Denotation, when dealing with artifacts, involves detailed descriptions and measurements. Connotation, on the other hand, involves the cultural meanings and myths connected to them. Let us consider an important artifact—a Barbie doll. From a denotation perspective, a Barbie doll is 11.5 inches tall and has the following measurements: 5.25 inches by 3 inches by 4 inches. It was invented in 1959. This material is all factual.

When we come to connotations of Barbie dolls then, we enter into the area of what these dolls symbolize about American culture and society, their cultural, symbolic, and mythic significance—matters that are quite controversial. Charles Winick in his book, *Desexualization in American Life,* offers an interpretation of the psychological and cultural significance of Barbie dolls and other dolls like Barbie. He suggests that Barbie dolls reflect a basic change in the way children are socialized. Instead of rehearsing for motherhood with baby dolls, little girls now learn how to become sexually attractive, practice how to have romantic relationships, and learn how to be consumers. If that is the case, Barbie dolls have changed the way girls develop and profoundly affected relationships between men and women. We see, then, that simple objects can reveal a great deal about many different aspects of the societies in which they are found and can have a profound impact on these societies.

The prototype teen or full-figured doll was introduced in 1957, and Barbie appeared in 1959, followed in two years by Ken, her male consort. Three Barbies have been sold for every Ken. An average of over six million mannequin dolls have been sold each year for a decade. A minimum standard wardrobe for Barbie costs an elegant $588. … What is the effect of these mannequin dolls on their millions of owners between four and twelve? Such girls may be much less able to achieve the emotional preparation for being a wife and mother that they received from baby dolls. Barbie is a sexy teenager. A girl who protects and sees her doll as a mother figure is seeing her mother as a teenager, which is certainly confusing. If the youngster identifies herself as the mother, then she is taking care of a child who is already an adolescent….

For the Barbie-weaned girl, a relationship with the opposite sex may not be marvelous and exciting; it could rather be a routinized aspect of our culture's material assembly line, lacking mystery or momentum because of its predictable outcome. The Barbie girl may learn to expect to be valued because of her ever-increasing wardrobe and ability to manipulate her father and, later, husband into buying clothes and more clothes. During the latency years, she is being introduced to precocious sexuality, voyeurism, fantasies of seduction, and conspicuous consumption.

Charles Winick, *Desexualization in American Life* (1995:226–227)

Winick's theory is that Barbie dolls, and other similar kind of dolls, reflect a basic change that took place in the socialization of young girls and led to a major change in the way girls thought about motherhood and their relationships to men. It is the connotations of Barbie dolls that are all important here. Barbie is, then, a signifier of considerable importance, and recognizing the signified aspects of these dolls is what is so revealing.

Conclusions

A semiotic approach to material culture offers us the ability to interpret objects and artifacts and, as the Barthes quote that begins this chapter shows, to explain how these objects tie in to cultural codes and such phenomena as the socialization of children and other social and cultural matters. It is important that we recognize that objects play varying roles in society, and their meaning is not exhausted in their immediate function. As Saussure pointed out, semiotics is the study of signs in society. We must not forget about this important aspect of semiotic theory which suggests that interpreting material objects can teach us a great deal about the societies in which they are found.

Everyday life is crisscrossed by patterns that regulate the behavior of its inhabitants with each other and that, at the same time, relate this behavior to much larger contexts of meaning (such as...canons of acceptable etiquette, the moral order and the sanctions of law). These regulatory patterns are what are commonly called institutions. Everyday life takes place within the enveloping context of an institutional order; it is intersected at different points by specific institutions that, as it were, reach into it, and its routines themselves consist of institutionalized behavior, that is, of behavior that is patterned and regulated in established ways. Again, it is important to understand the reciprocal relationship of these two aspects of our experience of society: everyday life can only be understood against the background of the specific institutions that penetrate it and of the overall institutional order within which it is located. Conversely, specific institutions and the institutional order as a whole are real only insofar as they are represented by people and by events that are immediately experienced in everyday life.

Peter L. Berger and Brigitte Berger,
Sociology: A Biographical Approach
(1972:10)

4.

Sociological Analysis of Material Culture

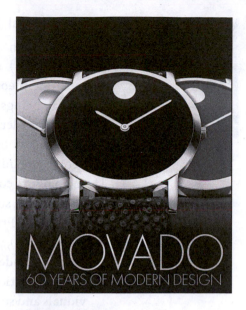

MOVADO
60 YEARS OF MODERN DESIGN

We've already dealt with two theoretical approaches to material culture: psychoanalytic theory and semiotic theory. To this list we now add sociological theory, which deals with attempts that sociologists and other scholars have made to understand how institutions, as described by the Bergers above, function in society. Sociology is, technically speaking, the study of human beings in groups and institutions. The focus is on the way society functions and includes such areas as marriage and the family, class systems, race, gender, religion, and other aspects of collective behavior. In this chapter I will focus on sociological theories and concepts that help illuminate material culture.

Sociological Theory

The French philosopher August Comte (1798–1857) used the term "sociology" to integrate theoretical and practical studies of human beings. His goal for sociology was "to know in order to predict in order to control." He wanted to discern the laws by which people organize their lives so he and other sociologists could help create a more humane and rational social order.

Another French scholar, Emile Durkheim (1858–1917), who is generally considered to be the founder of French sociology, argued that the relationship that exists between individuals and society is very complicated. As he explained in his book, *The Elementary Forms of Religious Life* (1915/1965:29):

> There are two beings in him: an individual being which has its foundation in the organism and the circle of whose activities is therefore strictly limited, and a social being which represents the highest reality in the intellectual and moral order that we can know by observation—I mean society. This duality of our nature has as its consequence in the practical order, the irreducibility of a moral ideal to a utilitarian motive, and in the order of thought, the irreducibility of reason to individual experience. In so far as he belongs to society, the individual transcends himself, both when he thinks and when he acts.

This helps explain what Peter and Brigitte Berger were writing about in the passage that opens this chapter. We have individuality, which is based on our physical endowments, the fact that we are an "organism," and we are also, at the same time, social beings, whose ideas and values are shaped, to varying degrees, by the social order.

We are in society and society is in us, and it is simplistic to neglect either of these two sides to our nature. We can say the same thing about artifacts: they are in society and society is reflected in them. That is why artifacts are not only reluctant witnesses to the past but also valuable witnesses to the present.

Functionalism

Many sociologists are structural-functionalists, who base their investigations on the notion that the institutions in society are part of an ongoing system of institutions, each of which is connected to all the others. They focus on whether an institution (or something else) helps contribute to the stability and maintenance of society, in which case the institution is "functional," or helps contribute to the destabilization and breakdown of society, in which case the institution is "dysfunctional" or "disfunctional." If an institution plays no role, it is "non-functional."

There is, we can see, a conservative bias to structural-functionalism, since it posits the maintenance of society as the primary consideration rather than focusing on change and the evolution of institutions and societies. We can also apply functionalism to components of institutions and to all kinds of different entities, including artifacts, asking what function the artifact has for people. Functionalists also distinguish between latent functions, which are not intended and of which we are not aware (but which may be very important), and manifest functions, which are intended and of which we are conscious.

The manifest function of cell phones is to be able to make phone calls just about everywhere. The latent functions of cell phones may involve anything from helping deal with loneliness and keeping track of children to making people feel powerful by being able to summon others at their command, so to speak, by punching a few numbers in a cell phone.

Our dependence on cell phones is so great that Barack Obama refused to give up his beloved Blackberry when he became president, and the secret service had to make arrangements so he could use it.

There are six aspects of functionalism that are of interest to theorists of material culture:

Functional	Helps maintain the entity
Dysfunctional	Helps destabilize the entity
Non-functional	Plays no role in the entity
Functional alternative	Substitutes for original function
Manifest function	Obvious, stated reason for using something
Latent function	Unconscious factors involved in using something

From a functionalist perspective, we can then ask a number of questions about artifacts. I will take smartphones as the subject for a functional analysis.

Aspects	Smartphone
Functional	connects with others
Dysfunctional	disturbs others, wastes time
Non-functional	n/a
Functional alternative	substitutes for traditional phone
Manifest function	makes phone calls, sends texts to other
Latent Function	controls others, avoids loneliness

The first signs of the next shift began to reveal themselves to me on a spring afternoon in the year 2000. That was when I began to notice people on the streets of Tokyo staring at their mobile phones instead of talking to them. The sight of this behavior, now commonplace in much of the world, triggered a sensation I had experienced few times before—the instant recognition that a technology is going to change my life in ways I can scarcely imagine. Since then the practice of exchanging short text messages via mobile telephones has led to the eruption of subcultures in Europe and Asia. At least one government has fallen, in part because of the way people used text messaging. Adolescent mating rituals, political activism, and corporate management styles have mutated in unexpected ways.

Howard Rheingold, *Smart Mobs: The Next Social Revolution* (2003:xi)

Rheingold's insight that smartphones would change the way we live has been born out as these devices and their smartphone successors have become ubiquitous and now play a major role in the social lives of young people all over the world. In many third world countries, cell phones and smartphones have enabled people to communicate with one another and connect to the internet for the first time, since there are few land lines or personal computers available.

We can see, then, that there is more to an object than its primary function, and the most interesting aspects of many kinds of material culture involve their covert and often unrecognized functions.

Taste Cultures

Sociologists and social scientists in all fields love to develop typologies—that is, classification schemes—that they believe help us better understand the way societies, institutions, and other phenomena function. One of the most interesting typologies was done by sociologist Herbert J. Gans in his book, *Popular Culture and High Culture.* Gans wanted to defend people who like popular culture against attack by elitists who like high or "elite" culture.

He did this by suggesting that in America (and by implication in other societies as well) there are a number of different popular cultures and elite cultures, and each of them is part of what he described as a taste culture. These taste cultures entertain us, inform us, and beautify our lives. As he explains (1974:10):

> Taste cultures, as I define them, consist of values, the cultural forms which express these values: music, art, design, literature, drama, comedy, poetry, criticism, news and the media in which these are expressed— books, magazines, newspapers, records, films and television programs, paintings

and sculpture, architecture, and insofar as ordinary consumer goods also express aesthetic values or functions, furnishings, clothes, appliances, and automobiles as well.

He then discusses the relationship between popular culture and elite culture and various problems associated with both, before offering a list of five American taste cultures. They are, he points out, very general and do not deal with religious, ethnic, and regional variants. His book was published in 1974, so many of his examples are dated or no longer exist, but Gans's theory, that there are five distinct taste cultures in America, offers us a way of thinking about who uses what kind of material culture.

Gans also points out that choices people make about the objects they purchase are connected to one another. That is, as he explains, people who read *The New Yorker* or *Harper's* also tend to like foreign films, listen to classical music, eat gourmet foods, and choose contemporary (once this was Danish modern) furniture.

These five American taste cultures are based on matters such as socio-economic class, religion, age, education, ethnic and racial background, and personality factors. They are listed below with examples of each. I have limited the examples to objects and material culture he mentions in his book:

1. High Culture
(socioeconomic-cultural elites, creative types)
Primitive Art and Abstract Expressionist Art
New York Review of Books

2. Upper Middle Culture
(executives, professionals, managers, and spouses)
Time, Newsweek
Harper's, New Yorker, Playboy, Ms, Vogue

3. Lower Middle Culture
(older lower-middle class people)
Hollywood Modern furniture (very ornate)
Confession magazines

4. Quasi-Folk Low Culture
(unskilled blue collar and service workers)
Tabloids
Comic books

5. Youth, Black, and Ethnic Cultures
Psychedelic and multimedia art
Tie-dyed and unisex clothing
Paraphernalia of drug culture

While we may question Gans's division of American consumers into five, and only five, taste cultures (or taste subcultures), it seems reasonable to suggest that there are a number of different somewhat amorphous cultural and socio-economic groupings in America, each of which has certain notions about what they like and don't like in art and, for our purposes, in the objects and artifacts they purchase.

What Gans does in his book is defend the different taste cultures and argue for aesthetic pluralism, pointing out that each of these taste cultures finds media and fashions appropriate to its interests, educational level, and aesthetic sensibilities. He tells us that the Lower Middle taste culture is the dominant one in America—or was in 1972 when he wrote his book.

The typology that Gans uses varies slightly from a classical portrait of American society made by W. Lloyd Warner 20 years before Gans wrote his book. In his 1953 book, *American Life: Dream and Reality,* Warner suggested that there are six classes in America:

Upper-Upper: 1.4%
Lower-Upper 1.6%
Upper-Middle 10%
Lower-Middle 28%
Upper-Lower 33%
Lower-Lower 25%

Arpege.
Very simply, the most beautiful gift in the world.

Arpege by **Lanvin**
Promise her anything, but give her Arpege.

He said that the Lower-Middle and Upper-Lower classes represent the common man and woman in America. Although these figures are more than 50 years old, they are not too far removed from the economic makeup of American society today, with the top one percent or so owning the lion's share of America's wealth.

A great deal of the reading we do in books and newspapers and magazines serves the purpose of giving us notions about what objects and other kinds of material culture are appropriate for individuals who are members of each socioeconomic class or taste culture. That is one of the functions of advertising, which teaches us how to evaluate objects and read people in terms of the objects they wear and own. Advertising teaches us to be "discriminating" consumers and to recognize what brands go with what kind of people.

For example, we generally scrutinize people we see (in real life, in movies, on television, in commercials and print advertisements) in terms of the brands they are wearing of products such as eyeglasses, sunglasses, shirts, ties, sweaters, coats, pants, jackets, shoes, sneakers, pocketbooks, briefcases, backpacks, and so on ad infinitum. Many of these products carry logos and other markers that people can see to facilitate the process. They are "status symbols," and will be discussed in the chapter on economics, Marxism, and material culture. One thing that wearing name brand and expensive brands seems to do is make us feel good about ourselves and about the image we project to others, because, in our minds, these name brand objects are indicators that we are successful. This leads to my next topic, the uses and gratifications that artifacts provide.

Uses and Gratifications Provided by Artifacts

The uses and gratification theory was developed, originally, by media theorists who were interested in why people listened to soap operas or watched certain television programs. Instead of trying to find out the effects of media usage, they focused on the uses people made of the media they consumed and the gratifications the various media genres provided. We can do the same thing for artifacts and theorize about the uses people make of the objects they have and the gratifications these objects have for them. To do this we have to modify the original list of uses and gratifications so they can be applied to the consumption and possession of artifacts.

To Have Beautiful Things

This is a variation of the gratification involved with experiencing the beautiful. There is a kind of psychological reward we get from having desired and beautiful things to wear and to have in the house, in that possessing "beautiful" or desired objects enhances a feeling of wellbeing in people and makes us feel that we have been successful.

To Find Diversion and Distraction

Here we find the process of purchasing objects enables us to escape from our mundane preoccupations in an effort to enhance—we believe—the quality of our lives. Also, the act of purchasing things gives us, if only for a short while, a sense of power and an escape from the anonymity that we find so troubling. And the objects we buy, such as smartphones, TVs, and tablets are often ones that we can use to entertain ourselves, though they may have other functions as well.

To Imitate Models We Respect

Many of the artifacts and products we purchase are due to a desire to imitate others. A French scholar, René Girard, has suggested in his book, *A Theater of Envy: William Shakespeare,* that we purchase things advertised using movie stars and celebrities because we imitate their desires, as reflected by their participation in advertisements and commercials.

To Affirm Aesthetic Values

Every choice we make of a tie, a shirt, a piece of jewelry or any other article of clothing or other kind of possession reflects our "taste," our aesthetic values and, in the case of conspicuous consumption, our status. We will see later, in the work done by Mary Douglas in the chapter on anthropology, that our choice of objects may be more connected to our lifestyles—the groups with which we identify—than to our personalities and taste.

Race, Ethnicity, and Gender

Race involves categorizing people by their genetic heritage. Traditionally, social scientists offered three racial categories: Negroid, Mongoloid, and Caucasian. This theory has come under attack in recent years by scholars who argue that race is not really a biological category but is, instead, a socially constructed one. And as more people from different races marry one another and have mixed-race children, the utility of race as a construct seems questionable.

Ethnicity refers to groups such as Jews, Italian-Americans, and Hispanics that share certain religious, racial, national, and cultural traits and cuisines. In some cases, such as the bagel, a food that originates with one ethnic group, Jews, becomes widely popular and loses its original ethnic identity. During a recent trip to Japan I saw bagels being sold in some bakeries.

It is possible to suggest that race and ethnicity play an important role in the choice of artifacts people purchase, and marketers have discerned that different races purchase different brands of alcohol, kinds of cigarettes, and food products. For example, African-Americans show a strong preference for menthol cigarettes (70 percent of African Americans prefer menthol cigarettes compared to 25 to 30 percent of white Americans), and Asian-Americans and Hispanics consume much more rice than Caucasians do.

Marketers use race and ethnicity to plan advertising campaigns. There is a book, *Racial and Ethnic Diversity: Asians, Blacks, Hispanics, Native Americans and Whites (5th edition)*, that marketers can purchase, along with another similar book, *Who's Buying by Race and Hispanic Origin*. Both of these books, and others on teenagers, women, and baby boomers, are published by New Strategist Publications.

There is some question as to whether race, age (generation), gender or socio-economic class or other factors are the dominant motivators behind the purchases of food products, clothes, and other artifacts and products people make. Some objects are gender specific, such as birth control pills (although there are now some made for men) and nylon stockings, and some objects migrate between genders, such as earrings, which used to be only worn by women but are now worn by many men as well.

Status

We can define status as the position an individual has in some group, or that a group has relative to other groups. One of the ways we demonstrate our status to others is by purchasing objects that function as status symbols, artifacts that suggest our wealth and socio-economic class. Sociologists suggest there are two kinds of status. The first kind, ascribed status, is based on factors such as our gender, our age, and the status of the family in which we are born. Achieved status is based on our merits, our abilities, and our success in various endeavors. Traditional societies are those in which ascribed status is dominant. In modern societies, achieved status tends to be the rule, but since some children are born into wealthy families and have better life chances than children born into poor families, achieved status means that many people who aren't financially successful suffer from alienation and a sense of relative deprivation.

Role

The concept of role is connected to status. Role refers to behavior expected of people who have a particular status. A person plays many different roles in the course of a day. A woman might be a mother, an executive in a corporation, and a member of a religious organization—three different roles. Our role behavior is generally unconscious, but sociologists have a concept, "dramatic role presentation," that deals with conscious efforts individuals make to create a positive impression among other people. For example, in a hierarchical institution such as a university, full professors have more status and play different roles than those played by associate professors and assistant professors.

A problem some individuals face is that they have not learned to play certain roles correctly, so, for example, young men and women who attend college and have not learned the correct roles to play as students often get into difficulties. We use the term "socialization" to refer to teaching people what roles to play in various situations in which they find themselves. Many people have been improperly socialized, which causes problems for them and others they come into contact with. Fashion is an area where one can display improper socialization, by wearing clothes that are not appropriate to one's status. It is important to know how to dress correctly or appropriately for various roles we are called upon to play.

Sociologists have discovered that some

people use fashion and other objects to imitate the behavior of groups with which they identify. Thus, there are groups of people who look like motorcycle riders because they wear leather jackets and other paraphernalia associated with motorcycle riding, but who don't own motorcycles. They are, as the semioticians would put it, "lying" with signs and symbols.

Jean Baudrillard's *The System of Objects*

Jean Baudrillard (1929–2007) was a French Marxist, sociologist, and semiotician, whose book, *The System of Objects* (1968 French edition/1996 English translation), is considered an important contribution to understanding material culture. In the introduction to the book he discusses his perspective on material culture (1996:3–4):

> Everyday objects (we are not concerned here with machines) proliferate, needs multiply, production speeds up the lifespan of such objects—yet we lack a vocabulary to name them all. How can we hope to classify a world of objects that changes before our eyes and arrive at an adequate system of description? There are almost as many criteria of classification as there are objects themselves: the size of the object; its degree of functionality (i.e., the object's relationship to its own objective function); the gestures connected with it (are they rich or impoverished? traditional or not?); its form; its duration; the time of day at which it appears...;

the material that it transforms...; the degree of exclusiveness or sociability attendant on its use (is it for private, family, public or general use?); and so on.

Baudrillard alerts us to the many different qualities of objects and the variety of roles they play in our lives—private and public. He provides us with a list of things to think about when we start analyzing objects. He adds, shortly after this passage, that he isn't interested in the functions of objects or the categories into which we may put them (1996:4) "but instead with the processes whereby people relate to them and with the systems of human behaviour and relationships that result therefrom." In other words, he is interested in what objects reveal about social relations and society in general.

In a chapter on advertising, Baudrillard calls our attention to the role that it plays in the way we think about and relate to objects. He writes (1996:164):

Any analysis of the system of objects must ultimately imply an analysis of discourse *about* objects—that is to say, an analysis of promotional "messages" (comprising image and discourse). For advertising is not simply an adjunct to the system of objects; it cannot be detached therefrom, nor can it be restricted to its "proper" function (there is no such thing as advertising strictly confined to supplying information). Indeed, advertising is now an irremovable aspect of the system of objects precisely by virtue of its disproportionateness.... Advertising in its entirety constitutes a useless and unnecessary universe. It is pure connotation. It contributes nothing to production or to the direct practical application of things, yet it plays an integral part in the system of objects, not merely because it relates to consumption but also because it itself becomes an object to be consumed.

When Baudrillard wrote his book, advertising may have had the role he gives it, but in recent years advertising agencies have actually played an important role in the design of objects as well as the effort to sell them to people. I have often thought that while many people know very little about American history, literature, or culture, they all have an enormous amount of "product knowledge" because they are exposed to so much advertising every day—on just about every flat surface available: television screens, computer monitors, cell phone screens, the sides of buses, and so on. As we shall see in John Berger's analysis of objects, advertising plays an all-important role in selling objects to people.

Conclusions

The sociological perspective offers some interesting insights into the role that objects and artifacts play in our lives, but it also raises some questions about how these objects function for people and what motivates people to purchase these objects. The functional perspective suggests that we cannot assume that we understand or recognize the roles the artifacts we purchase play in our lives, that quite often there are unrecognized functions played by artifacts and a multitude of different factors shaping our desire to choose and possess this or that artifact.

Sociological theory also suggests that we consider such factors as age, gender, race, social roles, status, and the uses and gratifications provided by objects when considering material culture. There are, then, a number of different sociological models and approaches we can use when dealing with material culture.

In the social production which men carry on they enter into definite relations that are indispensable and independent of their will; these relations of production correspond to a definite state of development of their material powers of production. The totality of these relations of production constitutes the economic structure of society— the real foundation, on which legal and political superstructures arise and to which definite forms of social consciousness correspond. The mode of production of material life determines the general character of the social, political and spiritual processes of life. It is not the consciousness of men that determines their being, but, on the contrary, their social being determines their consciousness.

Karl Marx, Preface to *A Contribution to the Critique of Political Economy* (1859:51)

5.

Economic Theory, Marxism, and Material Culture

If artifacts are simple objects showing human workmanship, it means that artifacts are made by others, either individual craftsmen or, what is more usually the case, large numbers of workers in huge factories in distant places. In contemporary America, many of the objects we purchase are made in China or other cheap labor countries. The object, then, is the tip of the iceberg, and below the seas, where we cannot see things clearly, there is human labor—labor that involves everything from designing objects, manufacturing them, transporting them, advertising them, and selling them.

Needs Versus Desires: Traveling Light and Arriving Heavy

Most of us have more "stuff" (to use George Carlin's term) than we need. How many pairs of pants, stockings, or shoes do we really need? The fact is, we tend to accumulate more

What Objects Mean, Second Edition by Arthur Asa Berger, 80–98. © 2014 Taylor & Francis. All rights reserved.

than we need or can use. Recently, I started thinking about all the "stuff" my wife and I have in our house: a piano, three sofas, a love seat, an old school bench, three leather Mexican chairs, two television sets, one of which is an LCD HDTV (20 inch), two desktop computers, two tablet computers, a dozen original oil paintings, one laptop computer, two cars, six clock-radios, eight pairs of old eyeglasses, three vacuum cleaners, three microwave ovens, five thousand books, three sets of china ware, two printers, one fax machine, one scanner, four telephones, a dishwasher, a washing machine, a dryer, a waste disposal system, four espresso machines, two coffee grinders, two MP3 players, two hi-fi sets, 200 CDs, and two cars...I could go on and on, and I haven't said anything about my other clothes or my wife's shoes, dresses, blouses, perfumes, or other things.

I haven't mentioned the brands of the various objects we own—a matter of considerable importance to many people, as we shall see. For it isn't only the objects you have that has to be considered; the brands of the objects are of major significance in the analysis of material culture. We can see the list of objects in my household, incomplete as it is, and from writer Rick Moranis's catalogue of his possessions, which I've only sampled, that it is easy to get lots of possessions and hard to get rid of them. "Get" is a nicer word than "buy" and doesn't suggest that you're paying money for things.

We all spend a good deal of time shopping, and when we shop we buy things—food, clothes, furniture, high-tech gizmos, CDs, stamps, cars... you name it. This stuff ends up in our houses, and so we spend our lives surrounded by objects of all kinds that we've purchased or have been given—what we might describe as the objects of our affection. Our shopping and the things we buy—or things that we are given and thus possess—are one way we define ourselves as persons to ourselves and to others, and we often develop strong emotional attachments to our possessions. That explains why we are so reluctant to part with them.

Rick Moranis on Material Culture

In a humorous article in the November 22, 2006, *New York Times,* writer Rick Moranis wrote a short essay, "My Days Are Numbered," in which he pointed out that he has:

5 television sets	4 printers
2 DVR boxes	2 non-working fax machines
3 DVD players	2 answering machines
19 remote controls	46 cookbooks
3 computers	68 take-out menus from 4 restaurants
5 sinks	2 refrigerators
26 sets of linen	506 CDs, cassettes, etc.
14 digital clocks	9 armchairs

Most of us don't have as many sinks, refrigerators, and take-out menus as Rick Moranis does, but if we make an inventory of our possessions, we're generally surprised at how much "stuff" we have accumulated.

Marxist Theory and Alienation

Karl Marx developed a number of economic and psychological theories to explain the role of capitalism in the modern world. One of the primary factors leading people to focus their attention on purchasing things is alienation, by which Marx meant a separation or estrangement of man's true nature from his sense of self. As he explained:

> Every man speculates upon creating a *new* need in another in order to force him to a new sacrifice, to place him in a new dependence, and to entice him into a new kind of pleasure and thereby into economic ruin. Everyone tries to establish over others an *alien* power in order to find there the satisfaction of his own egoistic need. (quoted in Fromm, 1962:50)

These "needs" are not real, Marxists argue, but are artificially imposed upon us by advertising agencies and marketers, who convince us we need to purchase this product or that gizmo if we are going to be really happy. We are alienated, Marx argues, because for most of us our work is "external" to us, and we only work so we can make money to live. As he wrote, "the life which he has given to the object sets itself against him as an alien and hostile force" (Fromm, 1962:170).

For Marxists, then, the objects and artifacts we possess are signifiers of the alienation we feel. We purchase things in order to assuage our sense of frustration with our situation—not recognizing, of course, why we are acting the way we do. Alienation, for Marx, affects everyone in bourgeois capitalist societies, not just workers. This would suggest, then, that the more artifacts we feel we need to have, the more we are signifying our alienation and the more alienated we are. So big diamond rings worn by wealthy women are, from a Marxist perspective, indicators of alienation and estrangement—from others and from oneself. When you have big diamond rings and other expensive artifacts, you always have to worry about losing them or people trying to take them away from you by one means or another.

Class Conflict

The unequal distribution of goods leads to class conflict, a basic Marxist theory. For Marx, history is the story of endless class conflict. As he writes (quoted in Bottomore and Rubel, 1964: 200):

> The history of all hitherto existing societies is the history of class struggles. Freeman and slave, patrician and plebeian, lord and serf, guild-master and journeyman, in a word oppressor and oppressed, stood in constant opposition to one another, carried on an uninterrupted, now hidden, now open, fight, a fight that each time ended either in a revolutionary reconstitution of society at large, or in the common ruin of the contending classes.

For Marx, the bourgeoisie, who own the means of production and form the ruling class, and the proletariat, who are the workers exploited by the bourgeoisie, are locked in a never-ending struggle. The ruling classes avert class struggle by indoctrinating the members of the proletariat with what Marx called "false consciousness," namely, ruling class ideas, such as the notion that everyone can succeed if they are willing to work hard enough (the "American Dream"). The ruling classes also avoid class conflict by making it possible for the proletariat to purchase goods and services that distract their attention from the class makeup of society and the unequal distribution of wealth.

The Role of Advertising

Advertising is for many Marxists the main engine of consumer culture in capitalist societies. It is not just a merchandizing tool but an industry that dominates everyday life and social relationships. A German Marxist, Wolfgang Haug, suggests in his book, *Critique of Commodity Aesthetics,* that the advertising industry has learned how to attach sexuality to objects and artifacts and to "aestheticize" them, enabling the ruling classes in capitalist societies to more fully exploit the masses. Advertising's immediate goal is to sell artifacts and various kinds of products, but its long range goal is to turn people's attention away from their exploitation and justify the existence of a capitalist economic system.

Another Marxist theorist, Henri Lefebvre, argues that it is advertising that gives all objects their valuation. As he writes in his book, *Everyday Life in the Modern World* (1971:105):

> In the second half of the twentieth century in Europe, or at any rate in France, there is *nothing*—whether object, individual or social group—that is *valued* apart from its double, the image that advertises and sanctifies it. This image *duplicates* not only any object's material, perceptible existence but desire and pleasure that it makes into fictions situating them in the land of make-believe, promising "happiness"— the happiness of being a consumer.

What advertising has done, Lefebvre believes, is transform itself from an industry inducing people to buy objects and products to one that gives them, and everything else, value and status in people's eyes. For Lefebvre, advertising has taken control of everyday life and gives everyone attitudes and a sense of style that inform their purchases and their lives.

An analysis of the system of objects must ultimately imply an analysis of discourse *about* objects—that is to say, an analysis of promotional "messages" (comprising image and discourse). For advertising is not simply an adjunct to the system of objects; it cannot be detached therefrom, nor can it be restricted to its "proper" function (there is no such thing as advertising strictly confined to the supplying of information). Indeed, advertising is now an irremovable aspect of the system of objects precisely because of its disproportioness. This lack of proportion is the "function" apotheosis of the system. Advertising in its entirety constitutes a useless and unnecessary universe. It is pure connotation. It contributes nothing to production or to the direct practical application of things, yet it plays an integral part in the system of objects, not merely because it relates to consumption but also because it itself becomes an object to be consumed.

Jean Baudrillard, *The System of Objects* (1996:164)

I discussed Baudrillard's book *The System of Objects* earlier. Here he stressed the importance of advertising, which convinces us to buy all these objects—most of which we don't really need. As advertising executives often explain, "our job is to convince you to buy things you didn't know you needed."

Thorstein Veblen and Conspicuous Consumption

Thorstein Veblen (1857–1929) was a "radical" American economist who offered a different perspective on the role of consumption in the United States. In his analysis of Veblen's theories, Lewis Coser writes in *Masters of Sociological Thought* (1971:268–269):

Veblen is at his best when he analyzes the various means by which men attempt to symbolize their high standing in the continuous struggle for competitive advantage. Conspicuous consumption, conspicuous leisure, conspicuous display of symbols of high standing are to Veblen some of the means by which men attempt to excel their neighbors and so attain heightened self-evaluation.

We must be mindful, Veblen tells us, of the ultimate goal of conspicuous consumption—namely, an enhanced sense of self.

Coser argues that Veblen uses functional analysis in dealing with conspicuous consumption. As Coser explains (1971:271):

When Veblen describes the various manifestations of the pattern of conspicuous consumption, he is always at pains to ferret out their latent functions. Manifestly, candles are meant to provide light and automobiles are means of transportation. But under the pecuniary scheme they serve the latent function of indicating and enhancing status. Candle light at dinner indicates that the host makes claims to a style of gracious living that is peculiar to the upper class....One serves caviar to symbolize the refinement of the palate that is the mark of a gentleman.

It is necessary, Veblen suggests, to look for the hidden or latent functions of objects to fully understand the role they play in our lives. The problem is that we can never feel satisfied with what we have. As Veblen writes in *The Theory of the Leisure Class*, "As fast as a person makes new acquisitions, and becomes accustomed to the new standard of wealth, the new standard forthwith ceases to afford appreciably greater satisfaction than the earlier standard did" (quoted in Coser 1971:268). This means we are locked into a situation in which we can never stop yearning for new and better things, because we are always comparing ourselves with others who have more than we do.

Max Weber and Calvinist-Protestant Thought

Max Weber (1864–1920), an important German sociologist and one of the founding fathers of sociology, argues that Calvinist theology is behind the development of capitalism and the attitudes people have towards their possessions. In his book, *The Protestant Ethic and the Spirit of Capitalism*, he makes a couple of important points relevant to our interests. The first involves what he describes as "worldly Protestant asceticism."

Calvin argues that people should discard the Catholic medieval ascetic perspective on life, which he sees as a philosophy that "malignantly deprives us of the lawful enjoyment of the Divine beneficence, but which cannot be embraced 'til it has despoiled man of all his senses and reduced him to a senseless block" (John Calvin, *Institutes of the Christian Religion*, quoted in Berger [2005:6]). We must distinguish, Calvin argues, between the ascetic extreme, which stresses abstinence and reduces life to its bare necessities, and its opposite, which involves gluttony and "fastidious-ness in our furniture, habitations, and our apparel" and other kinds of behavior that distract people from their religious obligations.

According to Max Weber, then, the "Protestant ethic" is behind the development of capitalism. Weber argues that the Protestant ethic loosened the grip on people's minds of medieval notions about the value of poverty and justified consumption as something that God wants people to do, something that has a divine significance. If people were to consume things, they needed money—so hard work had to be glorified, and wasting time on non-productive pursuits attacked. Weber uses the term *asceticism* to describe the Protestant perspective on life, but it is a different kind of asceticism from the medieval, self-denying asceticism that Calvin had disparaged.

In addition to providing a hard working and diligent workforce, the Protestant ethic convinced people that their place in the scheme of things had been settled by God. As Weber explains:

> The power of religious asceticism provided him [the bourgeois business man]... with sober, conscientious, and unusually diligent workmen, who clung to their work as to a life purpose willed by God. Finally, it gave him the comforting assurance that the unequal distribution of the goods of this world was a special dispensation of Divine Providence, which in these differences, as in particular grace, pursued secret ends unknown to men. (1958:177)

This belief that there is a "Divine Providence" that justifies the unequal distribution of wealth is a great comfort to those who form the ruling class, since it justifies their position and lifestyle. And since Divine Providence determines our economic fate, efforts to ameliorate the lives of the poor are fruitless. At the conclusion of his book, Weber discusses the ideas of Richard Baxter, a Puritan minister, who believed that "the care for external goods should only lie on the shoulders of the 'saint like a light cloak, which can be thrown aside at any moment.' But fate decreed that the cloak should become an iron cage" (Weber, 1958:181). Weber concludes his book arguing that "material goods have gained an increasing and finally an inexorable power over the lives of men as at no previous period of history" (1958:181). Our passion to possess objects and artifacts now dominates our lives and has reached its highest level, he suggests, in the United States, where stripped of its religious basis, it has become something with the character of sport.

It is reasonable to suggest that although overtly we have cast off the religious notions of the Calvinists, in the thinking of many people there still lingers a residue of the belief that those who have wealth are blessed by God. The love of external goods, the passionate desire to have things, and not just anything but the newest and most desirable things, has, it would seem, become Baxter's iron cage in which most people now find themselves trapped.

Georg Simmel on Fashion

The German sociologist Georg Simmel (1858–1918) offers us an insight into the role fashion plays in the economy. He talks about clothing, but fashion can be considered more broadly and understood to deal not only with new clothing styles but also with the development of the new models of artifacts we use. As he explains in his essay, "The Philosophy of Fashion" (quoted in David Frisby and Mike Featherstone, 1997:192):

The essence of fashion consists in the fact that it should always be exercised by only a part of a given group, the great majority of whom are merely on the road to adopting it. As soon as a fashion has been universally adopted, that is, as soon as anything that was originally done only by a few has really come to be practiced by all—as is the case in certain elements of clothing and in various forms of social conduct—we no longer characterize it as fashion. Every growth of a fashion drives it to its doom, because it thereby cancels out its distinctiveness.

Simmel points out an interesting process here: as soon as the exclusivity of a fashion becomes tainted by mass adoption, fashionistas and new adopters have to move on to something new. So there is a never ending chain of activity as items that are fashionable lose their distinctiveness when other items are created or newer versions are adopted, only to be replaced in turn by newer items. And capitalist economies are more than willing to create new products (such as MP3 players) and new versions of products (such as the iPod).

He also explains why women are so conscious of fashion. He maintains that it is because of their social and political subservience that women pay so much attention to fashion. As he writes (1997:196):

> Out of the weakness of social position to which women were condemned through the greatest part of history there arises their close relationship to all that is "custom," to that which is "right and proper," to the generally valid and approved form of existence. For those who are weak steer clear of individualization; they avoid dependence upon the self, with its responsibilities and the necessity of defending oneself unaided. Those in a weak position find protection only in the typical form of life.

So fashion consciousness, Simmel explains, has been a means by which women try to deal with their subservience and social and political weakness. Whether or not women are in fact such a group, we could say about all groups who are socially and economically marginal or weak that fashion plays an important role in their lives, though in some cases rather than blending in, they move in the opposite direction and use fashion to call attention to themselves.

Walter Benjamin and the Work of Art in the Age of Mechanical Reproduction

Walter Benjamin (1892–1940) was a German Marxist critic who was interested in the impact of mass production on objects. In a highly influential essay, "The Work of Art in the Age of Mechanical Reproduction," Benjamin dealt with what he described as the loss of "aura" in mass produced objects. He begins his essay with a discussion of mass production of works of art (in Gerald Mast and Marshall Cohen,1974:613):

> In principle a work of art has always been reproducible. Man-made artifacts could always be imitated by man. Replicas were made by pupils in practice of their craft, by masters for diffusing their works, and finally by third parties in pursuit of gain. Mechanical reproduction of a work of art, however, represents something new.

He then discusses a number of topics related to the matter of reproduction, including lithography and photography, pointing out that authenticity relies upon the presence of originals, which are a prerequisite for an object to be authentic. This led to a discussion of what Benjamin calls "auras." As he explains (1974:616):

The authenticity of a thing is the essence of all that is transmissible from its beginning, ranging from its substantive duration to its testimony to the history which it has experienced. Since the historical testimony rests on the authenticity, the former, too, is jeopardized by reproduction when substantive duration ceases to matter. And what is really jeopardized when the historical testimony is affected is the authority of the object.

One might subsume the eliminated element in the term "aura" and go on to say: that which withers in the age of mechanical reproduction is the aura of the work of art. This is a symptomatic process whose significance points beyond the realm of art. One might generalize by saying: the technique of reproduction detaches the reproduced object from the domain of tradition.

What Benjamin argues is that reproduced objects, or in the case of brand name artifacts, imitations or reproductions (and fakes), are separated from the "auras" of original works and from tradition. Once authenticity becomes irrelevant, he suggests, art no long is based on ritual with its focus on the creative artist and the creative process.

Most of the essay is concerned with film, which explains why it is reproduced in a book on film theory. But Benjamin's notion about auras can be applied, with a slight twist, to all manner of artifacts, especially name brand ones like watches, handbags, perfumes, and clothing. One of the things that the person who owns the original painting by Jason Berger is purchasing, from Benjamin's point of view, is Berger's aura, his spirit, which is an important selling point.

When people purchase name band products, they are, in reality, purchasing the aura, the good name that becomes attached to the creator of the product or the brand. The names of the creators of these artifacts are recognizable by their use of initials or logos found on such artifacts as sunglasses, wrist watches, handbags, jeans, cell phones, and fountain pens. There exists a vast industry of knock offs that appropriate the logos of name-brand products but lack the aura of the real versions of these artifacts. For the people who use these knock offs, the fact that they are using imitations is of little concern.

Authenticity and Postmodern Thought

One reason for this lack of concern about authenticity is because the concept is largely irrelevant in postmodern times. Postmodernism is an extremely complicated concept, but it has a number of central concerns, such as the notion that the overarching metaphysical systems that we used to believe in are no longer considered important. As the French scholar Jean-François Lyotard puts it, postmodernism is characterized by "incredulity toward metanarratives," the grand philosophical systems that we once used to order our lives. Postmodernism also dissolves the boundaries between elite culture and popular culture and between original works of art and reproductions or imitations. So authenticity is not considered important in postmodern thought.

The postmodernists argue that contemporary American culture is postmodern. They suggest that around 1960 there was a huge cultural swing from modernist thought, which valued the great metanarratives and authenticity, to postmodern thought, which mixes styles and adopts the pastiche as a cultural dominant. In postmodern societies,

then, knock offs are perfectly acceptable, even desired, since they are a great deal less expensive than name brand originals.

John Berger on Advertising and Material Culture

John Berger is a British Marxist, who wrote a book (based on a series of BBC television shows) called *Ways of Seeing* (1978). It deals with painting and other elite arts, but also has a chapter on advertising—or what he calls "publicity." As he explains (131–132):

> Publicity is not an assembly of competing messages: it is a language in itself which is always being used to make the same general proposal. Within publicity, choices are offered between this cream and that cream, that car and this car, but publicity as a system only makes a single proposal.

It proposed to each of us that we transform ourselves, or our lives, by buying something more. This more, it proposes, will make us, in some way richer—even though we will be poorer by having spent our money.....Publicity is effective precisely because it feeds upon the real. Clothes, food, cars, cosmetics, baths, sunshine are real things to be enjoyed in themselves. Publicity begins by working on a natural appetite for pleasure....Publicity is never a celebration of a pleasure-in-itself. Publicity is always about the future buyer. It offers him an image of himself made glamorous by the product or opportunity it is trying to sell. The image then makes him envious of himself as he might be. Yet what makes this self-which-he-might-be enviable? The envy of others. Publicity is about social relations, not objects.

The point the Berger makes, that publicity is about social relations, is a bit misleading. What he is arguing, I would suggest, is that the objects we purchase play an important role in our social relations and that advertising is the engine that gives the objects we purchase their significance for us.

Conclusions

The objects and artifacts that play such an important role in our everyday lives—our cell phones, our digital watches, our blue jeans, our running shoes, and all the other items that we buy, can be understood by Marxists to be the means by which ruling classes distract Americans from recognizing their domination and the grossly unfair unequal distribution of wealth and income in this country. The fact that people who are not wealthy can purchase knock offs of the name brand products purchased by wealthy people may be functional for the ruling classes, since these knock offs allow people to imitate the consumption patterns of the ruling elites in societies.

Sociologists Weber and Simmel are not Marxists, but they recognize the importance of material goods to people as giving them a sense of their value and goodness. Weber discusses material culture more broadly, tying our love of things to Calvinism and Protestant thought and an attack on medieval asceticism. Simmel focuses upon fashion, explains it is a social force based upon differentiation, and links women's concern with fashion to their social subjugation.

Baudrillard offers a semiotically informed analysis of various kinds of material culture in his book, *The System of Objects,* and points out the important role advertising has in consumer cultures. Walter Benjamin, another German thinker, calls our attention to the "auras" that he alleges distinguish original works of art from imitations. This focus on originality and auras raises the question of authenticity and the postmodern perspective on culture, which argues that authenticity is irrelevant in contemporary societies, since the distinctions between original/imitation and elite/pop culture are held as spurious.

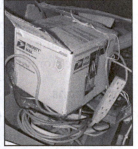

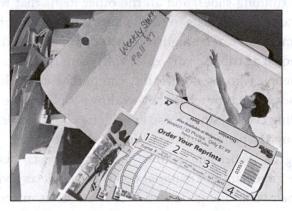

All theories of the past rely implicitly upon some concept of human nature: why humans behave the way we do, and how our behavior relates to our social and physical environment. In culture historical views, humans primarily act to reproduce their peculiar cultural traditions; in functionalist views humans act in response to environmental conditions to maximize their chances of survival.... Material culture studies: like the body, material things are a medium through which we create ourselves and understand other people, and hence an inescapable element of social reproduction. Artefacts are a key to social relations and frames of mind. Indeed, there has been considerable debate among archaeological theorists about whether things can be considered as agents in the same way that people can. Among the many ways in which material things relate to agency, we may note particularly technology as a system of social knowledge and embodied action, the use of everyday things to communicate subtle political meanings such as the authority of the state, the contextual use of material things to redefine or contest inherited meanings, and the question of the extent to which the archaeological record might be an intentional creation.

John Robb, in Colin Renfrew and
Paul Bahn, eds., *Archaeology: The Key
Concepts* (2005)

6.
Cultural Theory and Material Culture

Anthropology, as its Greek roots suggest, is the study of man, or as we would now say, human beings, so we can include women in the definition. Literally it means (*logos*) words (*anthropo*) about man or human beings. It is generally defined as the scientific study of the physical, social, and cultural development of man. There are different branches of anthropology, such as cultural (or social) anthropology, which deals with the analysis of social life and the relationship that exists between culture and personality, and linguistic anthropology that focuses upon language. Archaeology is a branch of anthropology that studies the past, often the very distant past, by using ancient artifacts and other materials.

The anthropological study of material culture found in this book is similar to archaeology, except that the focus is on more contemporary times, objects, and artifacts with which most of us are familiar, and it uses a multi-disciplinary approach to the subject. The central concept in anthropological theory is culture, a term that has been defined in numerous ways by social scientists over the years. The importance of culture is dealt with in the quotation with which this chapter begins.

Culture

Earlier in the book I offered a definition of culture that suggested that many cultural values and beliefs are incorporated into or reflected by material culture, which explains why we can learn so much from the artifacts and objects that play such an important role in our lives. But interpreting the meaning of these artifacts is a problem. As Stuart Hall explains in his book, *Representation: Cultural Representations and Signifying Practices* (1997:2–3):

> What has come to be called the "cultural turn" in the social and human sciences, especially in cultural studies and the sociology of culture, has tended to emphasize the importance of *meaning* to the definition of culture. Culture, it is argued, is not so much a set of *things*—novels, paintings or TV programmes and comics—as a process, a set of *practices*. Primarily, culture is concerned with the production and exchange of meanings...between the members of a society or group...The emphasis on cultural practices is important. It is participants in a culture who give meaning to people, objects and events. Things "in themselves" rarely if ever have any one single, fixed and unchanging meaning...It is by our use of things, and what we say, think and feel about them—how we represent them—that we give *them a meaning*.

Hall deals with some important concerns. He emphasizes that culture is now of major importance in the social and human sciences and points out that what is important is that we focus on the meanings that people give to objects—meanings that are varied, can change in time, and should be studied by many different disciplines.

Clotaire Rapaille on Culture Codes

Clotaire Rapaille, an anthropologist and market researcher, published a bestselling book in 2006 called *The Culture Code: An Ingenious Way to Understand Why People Around the World Live and Buy As They Do*. His basic argument is that culture can be thought of as a series of codes that we learn while we grow up and that shape our behavior in many different areas. He writes that young children, up to the age of seven, become imprinted with the beliefs and attitudes most central to them in the culture or subculture in which they are raised. He calls a combination of experiences and accompanying emotions "imprints" and explains that once children receive an imprint, that imprint, at an unconscious level, shapes their attitudes towards food, artifacts, automobiles and all the other things they buy or own. As he explains (2006:10–11):

> All of the different codes for all of the different imprints, when put together, create a reference system that people living in these cultures use without being aware of it. These reference systems guide different cultures in very different ways.

An imprint and its code are like a lock and its combination. If you have all the right numbers in the right sequence, you can open the lock. Doing so over a vast array of imprints has profound implications. It brings us to the answer to one of our most fundamental questions: why do we act the way we do? What's more it confirms what we have always suspected is true—that despite our common humanity, people around the world really *are* different. *The Culture Code* offers a way to understand how.

His book is full of examples of how cultural codes shape people's behavior. One interesting example involves the difference between American and French attitudes towards cheese. For the French, the code for cheese is alive, so they store it in a cloche, a bell shaped object with holes that allows air in and keeps bugs out. Americans, on the other hand, code cheese as dead, and so they store cheese in "plastic (like body bags), and store it, still wrapped air tight, in a morgue known as a refrigerator" (2006:25).

Rapaille believes that in addition to the Freudian individual unconscious and the Jungian collective unconscious there is a third "cultural" unconscious which explains why there is a French mind, an American mind, an English mind, and so on—minds that shape the way we purchase things and our attitudes toward the things we purchase. In his book he has interesting and provocative things to say about alcohol, food, and luxury products. What the culture code concept suggests is that every artifact reflects certain national, cultural, or subcultural attitudes and values that have been imprinted on young children growing up in a given culture. We can, in many

cases, use artifacts, then, as a means of discerning these hidden codes. Culture codes provide us with one more means of understanding material culture.

To this discussion we might add the notion that the codes often suggest "correct" combinations of foods or other objects. For example, consider the "classic" American steak dinner. American food codes suggest that steaks are to be grilled or broiled, but never boiled. The idea of boiling a sirloin steak strikes us as repugnant—a waste of good red meat. Upscale taste canons also tell us that the steak should be rare, possibly medium rare, and most certainly not well done. We have certain vegetables with steak: spinach, baked potatoes or French fries, and never boiled potatoes or beets or Brussels sprouts. This steak dinner code is reflected in countless menus in restaurants all over America and is internalized by young Americans as they grow up learning to associate certain tastes with steak.

Mary Douglas and Grid-Group Theory

Social anthropologist Mary Douglas offers a different perspective on why people buy the things they do or are given the things they have: grid-group theory, which she developed over the course of her long and distinguished career. According to Douglas, the objects and services that we buy and possess (as gifts, inheritances, and so forth) are culturally defined and best understood as being tied to our lifestyles. As she explains in her essay, "In Defence of Shopping," there are four, and only four, mutually hostile lifestyles. These lifestyles have been described by Aaron Wildavsky, a political scientist who often collaborated with Douglas, using slightly different language, as elitist (sometimes hierarchical elitist), individualist, egalitarian, and fatalist, and everyone in modern democratic societies belongs to one of them. Individualists and elitists are the dominant groups in most societies, and the egalitarians exist to critique the shortcomings of these two groups and attempt to raise up the fatalists from their lowly position.

It is our membership in one of these lifestyles, grid-group theorists argue, that shapes our behavior as consumers, and thus the objects we have in our houses reflect the lifestyle to which we belong. Members of each of these lifestyles aren't generally conscious of their membership in them, but they do recognize that they are different from, and are antagonistic to, other lifestyles that "do not have our kind of people in them." It is our membership in lifestyles or groups, then, that is basic in shaping our tastes and our sense of style.

Grid-group theory argues that individuals in all societies have to decide who they are (what group they belong to) and what they should do (follow the rules of the group or neglect them). Groups have either weak or strong boundaries and many or few prescriptions or rules. We then find there are four possibilities as reflected in the chart below:

		Group Strength of Boundaries	
		Weak	Strong
Grid Rules & Prescriptions	Many	Fatalists	Elitists Hierarchical Elitists
	Few	Individualists	Egalitarians

Another way to see these relationships is in the table that follows. The point is that if group membership and rules are the two dimensions, you can only have four lifestyles. In the realm of politics, Wildavsky calls these lifestyles "political cultures." When we vote, we make our decisions based on the hidden imperatives found in our political culture.

Boundaries	Prescriptions	Lifestyle
Weak	Many and binding	*Fatalists*
Weak	Few	*Individualists*
Strong	Many and binding	*Hierarchical Elitists*
Strong	Few	*Egalitarians*

Social scientists Michael Thompson, Richard Ellis, and Aaron Wildavsky explain in their book, *Cultural Theory*, how the four cultures are derived:

Strong group boundaries coupled with minimal prescriptions produce social relations that are egalitarian....When an individual's social environment is characterized by strong group boundaries and binding prescriptions, the resulting social relations are hierarchical [sometimes known as hierarchical elitist]...Individuals who are bounded by neither group incorporation nor prescribed roles inhabit an individualistic social context. In such an environment all boundaries are provisional and subject to negotiation...People who find themselves subject to binding prescriptions and are excluded from group membership exemplify the fatalistic way of life. Fatalists are controlled from without. (1990:6–7)

Grid-group theory enables us to understand many of the things we do with a new light and a new understanding.

Douglas explains her ideas about how grid-group theory applies to shopping and purchasing things in her important defense of shopping article mentioned above in Pasi Falk and Colin Campbell's *The Shopping Experience*. She writes (1997: 17–18):

Consumption behavior is continuously and pervasively inspired by cultural hostility...We have to make a radical shift away from thinking about consumption as a manifestation of individual choices. Culture itself is the result of myriads of individual choices, not primarily between commodities but between kinds of relationships. The basic choice that a rational individual has to make is the choice about what kind of society to live in. According to that choice, the rest follows. Artefacts are selected to demonstrate the choice. Food is eaten, clothes are worn, books, music, holidays, all the rest are choices that conform with the original choice for a form of society. Commodities are chosen because they are not neutral; they are chosen because they would not be tolerated in the rejected forms of society and are therefore permissible in the preferred form. Hostility is implicit in their selection.

The comment by Douglas that shopping is "a struggle to define not what one is but what one is not" suggests that it is our membership in one of the four cultures or lifestyles that shapes our consumer preferences. So the artifacts and objects that we purchase are not, Douglas asserts, based on personality and taste but on our membership in a culture or lifestyle, which silently and covertly dictates our choices.

Of course, Douglas may not be correct, but her article and her theory of grid-group relations pose a challenge to everyone who believes that people purchase things based on their distinctive personalities, taste, and sense of style. These matters, Douglas suggests, are culturally determined and connected to one of the four lifestyles to which people belong. What we buy is not, she argues, the expression of individual wants and desires but the expression of our cultural alignments.

It is possible to use grid-group theory to explain different lifestyle choices in media and in material culture. Every artifact and object we buy, which means much of what we buy (excluding services and certain very expensive things like houses), can be placed in one of the four lifestyles. For example, if we take songs as our topic, we can suggest that Hierarchical Elitists would prefer "God Save the Queen," Individualists would like "I Did It My Way," Egalitarians would like "We Are the World," and Fatalists would like "Que Sera, Sera." When we deal with artifacts and objects using grid-group theory, we find the following:

Object	Elitist	Individualist	Egalitarian	Fatalist
Books	*The Prince*	*Looking Out for Number One*	*I'm Okay, You're Okay*	*Down and Out in Paris and London*
Men's clothes	Military Uniforms	Suits	Blue Jeans	Thrift Store
Games	Chess	Monopoly	Frisbee	Russian Roulette
Magazines	*Architectural Digest*	*Money*	*Mother Jones, The Nation*	*Soldier of Fortune*

Many of these placements were suggested by students in classroom exercises in which they were asked to place objects and media texts in the correct slot. There are many brands of objects that could be placed in the four slots, and some of the placements are open to debate. What struck me when I played this learning game with my students was how much product knowledge they had about brands of cars, perfumes, and other artifacts. But that's to be expected in a country that spends around 150 billion dollars a year on advertising. From this perspective, newspapers and magazines can be looked upon as similar to textbooks for people, teaching them about the artifacts that are important parts of their lives: cell phones, MP3 players, jeans, and so on.

Myth and Material Culture

Myths can be defined as sacred narratives that shape cultural values and behavior. We find an excellent and more elaborated definition of myth in Raphael Patai's *Myth and Modern Man*. He describes myth in the following terms (1972:2):

> Myth...is a traditional religious charter, which operates by validating laws, customs, rites, institutions and beliefs, or explaining sociocultural situations and natural phenomena, and taking the form of stories, believed to be true, about divine beings and heroes.

He adds that myths play an important role in shaping social life and that "myth not only validates or authorizes customs, rites, institutions, beliefs, and so forth, but frequently is directly responsible for creating them" (1972:2). Marcel Danesi, who has written extensively on semiotics, media, and popular culture, offers another description of myth. He writes in his book, *Understanding Media Semiotics* (2002:47–48):

> The word "myth" derives from the Greek *mythos:* "word," "speech," "tale of the gods." It can be defined as a narrative in which the characters are gods, heroes, and mystical beings, in which the plot is about the origin of things or about metaphysical events in human life, and in which the setting is a metaphysical world juxtaposed against the real world. In the beginning stages of human cultures,

myths functioned as genuine "narrative theories" of the world. That is why all cultures have created them to explain their origins.... The use of mythic themes and elements in media representations has become so widespread that it is hardly noticed any longer.... Implicit myths about the struggle for Good, of the need for heroes to lead us forward, and so on and so forth, constitute the narrative underpinnings of TV programmes, blockbuster movies, advertisements and commercials, and virtually anything that gets "media air time."

Not only do myths pervade our media and popular culture, of particular interest to us is the fact that they are found in advertisements for products that play such an important part in our lives.

I would suggest that many myths can be found behind the various artifacts we use, though the mythic origins of these artifacts may not be evident to us. The impetus for my work on myths was Mircea

Eliade, who wrote in *The Sacred and the Profane* that many things that people do in contemporary society are actually camouflaged or modernized versions of ancient myths and legends. As he explains (1961:204–205):

> The modern man who feels and claims that he is nonreligious still retains a large stock of camouflaged myths and degenerated rituals... A whole volume could well be written on the myths of modern man, on the mythologies camouflaged in the plays that he enjoys, in the books that he reads. The cinema, that "dream factory," takes over and employs countless mythological motifs— the fight between hero and monster, initiatory combats and ordeals, paradigmatic figures (the maiden, the hero, the paradisal landscape, hell, and so on).

Eliade defines myth, I should add, as the recitation of a sacred history, "a primordial event that took place at the beginning of time" (1961:95).

Let me offer, here, a number of myths that relate to contemporary material culture and apply them to material culture. My argument, based on Eliade's point about unrecognized myths permeating our culture and Patai's notion that myths help shape culture, is that there are camouflaged and unrecognized myths that inform many of our behaviors and that are behind many of the things we purchase. The implication is that when we buy artifacts, our behavior is related to ancient myths, and thus, through these objects that we desire and purchase, we live mythically, even if we may not recognize that such is the case. The same applies to many objects that are given to us by others.

Myth	Material Culture
Mercury/Hermes	Running shoes
Pan	MP3s, online music streaming
Bacchus/Dionysus	Wine
Medusa	Shampoo
Cupid	Perfume
Ariadne	GPS-enabled devices

Mercury was the god with winged feet who flew as swift as thought. You can see the connection between him and the expensive running shoes people purchase, which they believe will enable them to run as fast as they can. Pan was a great musician who played reed pipes to charm everyone. A smartphone playing MP3s or streaming music can be seen as a portable Pan that plays music the owner likes. Bacchus, also known as Dionysus, was the god of wine, who gave to his followers either ecstatic joy or brutality—familiar after effects of those who imbibe too much wine or other alcoholic spirits. Medusa was the goddess whose hair killed all those who gazed on her. We can modify things and suggest that women who use shampoos and other hair products hope to have a powerful effect ("knock 'em dead") on men who see them. I call this notion women have that their hair can be all powerful as a means of attracting attention of others the "Medusa Complex." Cupid was the god of love who shot arrows that made those who were shot fall in love. His love arrows functioned the same way women think perfume does, making those who smell the perfume become sexually attracted to the woman or man (now that men wear so many fragrances) wearing it.

Ariadne was a princess, the daughter of King Minos of Crete; she gave a ball of thread to Theseus, who went into the Labyrinth in Crete to slay the minotaur. Theseus attached the thread at the entrance and rolled it out as he walked around in the Labyrinth. The Minotaur was a half bull, half human monster that was imprisoned in the Labyrinth and was given a yearly tribute of seven maidens and seven youths to devour. Theseus killed the Minotaur and, thanks to the thread he had unwound, found his way out of the Labyrinth. After escaping from the Labyrinth, Theseus eloped with Ariadne but abandoned her on the island of Naxos, because of his interest in another woman. She then formed a relationship with Dionysus. We can suggest that GPS devices and GPS-enabled smartphones are similar in function to Ariadne's ball of thread and that cities are in various ways analogous to labyrinths.

The Myth Model and Material Culture

Many of the objects we purchase can be connected to certain myths, as I've just demonstrated. But these objects can also be seen as being connected to what I describe as the "myth model," which, I suggest, shapes much of our behavior. I suggest that we can find myths in psychoanalytic theory, in various historical events, in elite culture, in popular culture, and in everyday life. Many of the things we do in everyday life, such as purchasing some object, are connected to ancient myths—though we are not aware of the connection. Below I offer an example of the myth model and the way a myth may be seen to be behind our purchasing an object.

Myth	Prometheus, who brings fire to mankind
Psychoanalytic Theory	Pyromaniacs
Historical events	Fires in forests
Elite Culture	Byron's poem about Prometheus
Popular Culture	The Human Torch
Everyday Life	Buy a cigarette lighter

We are not aware of the relationship between our actions and ancient myths, but the myth model shows us—at least in the examples offered—that many of the things we do are based ultimately on what Eliade described as camouflaged myths.

Mark Gottdiener on Cultural Studies

In his book, *Postmodern Semiotics: Material Culture and the Forms of Postmodern Life*, sociologist Mark Gottdiener offers a discussion of objects in a section devoted to "Cultural Studies" (1995:165–166):

> The analysis of mass culture involves a three-way relationship among (1) cultural objects that are produced by the industrial process, (2) a set of institutions that produce and distribute such objects on a relatively large scale, and (3) a collectivity(ies) or social group(s) of those who use such objects in contexts that can include use within a creative or connotatively polysemic setting. A mass cultural "object" can include everything from perceptual products (a television program) to highly subjective experiences (Disneyland). The distinguishing characteristics of mass cultural forms are found in the means by which these objects are produced and distributed—that

is, by the mass marketing industries—and in the nature of their use primarily, though not exclusively, for entertainment. Finally, the contents of mass cultural production involves people or events in society as well as the objects themselves.

Gottdiener uses the term "object" in a broader way than I do in this book, but his stress on the importance of mass marketing calls our attention, once again, to the role that advertising plays in the way we think about and use objects. The cultural studies perspective, as I understand it, is one that uses semiotics, psychoanalytic theory, Marxist theory, sociological theory, and whatever other theory is available to help us make sense of the cultural significance of objects.

Conclusions

The anthropological perspective on artifacts focuses on the role culture plays in their creation and use. According to Rapaille there are culture codes found in different countries and numerous subcultures that shape our attitudes towards many objects. The example used was cheese, but it applies to many other artifacts. Social anthropologist Mary Douglas argues that in modern countries there are four mutually hostile lifestyles that shape our behavior and consumption patterns, so the artifacts we purchase are not really individual decisions based on our personalities and taste. Finally, it was suggested that there are camouflaged and modernized versions of myths that can be found in many of our behaviors and that can be linked to many of the artifacts we use.

We must also keep in mind that an object has different meanings and valuations in different cultures, that the "figure" takes its meaning from the "ground" in which it is found. For example, a pair of original Levi's may suggest "cowboy" in the American west but may suggest an elite status in Japan or Russia. In the same light, an old Cadillac means something different in an affluent suburb and in a depressed section of a city.

Objects can act as symbols encapsulating the beliefs of a given culture at a particular moment in time through their physical form and decoration. This is often preserved through the object's continued survival and is referenced for future generations. Thus objects should be seen as palimpsests, having an evolving series of meanings over time...The appreciation of objects as containing a range of information is exemplified in Hodder's assertion...that objects can be seen as possessing three forms of identity:

- In use, functioning and having an effect on the world.

- The symbolic meaning of the object, its role in the cultural code; as such every object echoes and reinforces the meanings of the codes of the culture.

- Embodying and signifying past experience: through its appearance it carries ideas and information about the past into the present.

Chris Caple, *Objects: Reluctant Witnesses to the Past*

7.
Archaeological Theory and Material Culture

Archaeology is defined in *The Random House Dictionary of the English Language* as "the scientific study of historic and prehistoric peoples and their cultures by analysis of their artifacts, inscriptions, monuments and other remains, especially those that have been excavated." In the popular media, there are many television shows that show archaeologists involved in digs, searching for objects that will help them gain insights into the way people lived in earlier times, and Indiana Jones films that suggest that archaeologists can have very exciting lives though they do not actively reflect contemporary archaeological practice.

We are all fascinated by the buildings ancient civilizations constructed, the objects they made, and their everyday lives, rituals,

What Objects Mean, Second Edition by Arthur Asa Berger, 118–130. © 2014 Taylor & Francis. All rights reserved.

and beliefs. As the quotation about Ian Hodder's theories that opens this chapter suggests, we can find many ways of interpreting the functions and symbolic meanings of the artifacts we discover.

Archaeologists have problems different from others who analyze material culture. Because they deal with objects of the past, they have no way of directly corroborating their guesses as to the meaning of objects to the culture they were found in. All the likely informants are dead. So archaeology has approached the study of material culture inferentially, spending more time investigating the production, distribution, and use of objects and using various methods to hypothesize their meaning.

Archaeological theory offers different perspectives on how to think about the ancient objects . In his book, *Archaeology: The Key Concepts,* Clive Gamble writes that there are three main thrusts or paradigms in archaeological theory: a cultural historical one, an anthropological (or processual) one, and a postmodern (or post-processual) one.

The Cultural History and Anthropological Archaeology Approaches

Gamble describes the cultural history approach to archaeology as follows (2005:22–23):

> On a world scale culture history accounts for what the majority of archaeologists think they are doing...its practitioners emphasize the primacy of data, facts and classification....Allied with this focus on facts is the notion that an inductive approach is best suited to archaeological enquiry. Putting things in the right order, chronologically and geographically, is the most important goal for the culture historian.

From the culture historical approach we have got terms such as "Neolithic" and "Basketmaker" that are widely used in archaeological practice. The culture history approach to archaeology has built up an impressive body of knowledge of archaeological sequences and related artifacts in many parts of the world, especially after the development of radiocarbon dating methods. We know where and when ancient cultures lived—even if we don't know what they called themselves—and what their key cultural elements were. The problem with the culture history approach is that it is primarily descriptive of cultures and their material, that it cannot account for either stability or change in ancient cultures in ways other than what we observe in the modern world. Having been developed in the age of European colonialism, it often uses the colonial experiences of modern countries to explain ancient lives.

Processual Theory

The perceived deficiencies of the culture history approach led a number of archaeologists in a different direction and to the development in the 1960s of what is called processual archaeology. It is generally held that this movement started with a seminal paper by Lewis Binford in 1962 titled "Archaeology as Anthropology." Gamble describes this new direction in archaeology as follows (2005:25–26):

This short paper was concerned with process, how the various cultural systems that made up a society fitted together and worked. It dealt with the issues of adaptation and change in such systems by identifying three realms of behavior—environmental, social and ideological—which could be inferred from artefacts and the contexts in which they were found. It stressed the importance of quantification and prediction to qualify archaeology as a scientific approach. Most importantly, it drove explanation out from behind its hiding place of common sense and tradition. Explanation, putting assumptions down and challenging them, was a key objective.

We can see that this approach is considerably different from the culture history approach in that it attempts to imitate the natural or hard sciences. Its focus is on explaining how adaptation and variation occur, why some cultures do not change, and it wants to avoid using the circular argument of employing the concept of culture to explain how cultures change.

Jeremy Sabloff offers more details about the agenda of processual archaeologists in his chapter on the subject in *Archaeology: The Key Concepts,* a book edited by Colin Renfrew and Paul Bahn. Sabloff explains Binford's agenda for processual archaeology as follows (2005:214–215):

> First, the processual archaeologists stressed that culture should be viewed as a system with its technological, economic, social, political and ideological aspects all closely intertwined. Second, they noted the importance of cultural ecology, and the necessity to view the interaction of the environment and culture systematically.... Third, they argued that archaeologists should study the evolution of these cultural systems through time.... More specifically, processual archaeologists emphasized the importance of developing explicit research strategy designs to further archaeological understanding of cultural processes.

Implied in this theory is the notion that archaeological research can help scholars understand cultural change and the various behaviors that generated the material record—the artifacts and objects that archaeologists use to try to better understand the cultures that created them. Because it deals with the general patterns of human behavior across time and space, this theory also suggests that archaeology can be of use to us in dealing with contemporary social issues and problems.

A number of archaeologists were not satisfied with the pronouncements of processual theory. While adding more elements of natural science to archaeological practice, it focused on middle range theory, which offered hypotheses on small problems—how people in a certain locale gathered their food or procured material for making tools—but ignored the big question of how the human species got to its present state. It also set the archaeologist up as a distant, objective white-coated scientist, looking through the cultures of world prehistory as through a microscope. This new generation of archaeologists, beginning in the 1980s, developed a counter-theory known as post-processual theory, to which we now turn.

Post-processual Theory

Also in *Archaeology: The Key Concepts,* Ian Hodder, one of the leading post-processual proponents and a professor of archaeology at Stanford University, writes (2005:209):

> The term "interpretive archaeology" was often used to define this more positive approach…. The emphasis on interpretation (rather than the processual emphasis on explanation) is that different people with different social interests will construct the past differently. There is thus an uncertainty and ambiguity in the scientific process that cannot simply be resolved by appeal to objective data, because what people see as objective data also varies…. Rather, interpretation involves a to-and-fro between data and theory as more and more bits of information are fitted together into a coherent argument—this fitting process is best described as

"hermeneutic." It allows some interpretations to be favoured over others and "best fits" to be identified.

Post-processual archaeologists highlighted the limits of archaeology as a science, showed the limits about what we know about the past, and highlighted how multiple interpretations are possible from the same object depending on the viewpoint of the observer.

All three theories—culture history, processualism, and post-processualism—are currently used by archaeologists, according to Hodder, to answer different questions. The old battles between processual and post-processual archaeologists have been abandoned, and archaeologists now use social theories from a variety of disciplines and theories (such as Marxism, Psychoanalytic theory, Feminism, and Postmodernism) when they are useful to the data they have collected and the problems they are interested in solving.

Archaeology's Contribution to Material Culture Theory

Because of the limitations in knowing the meaning of objects to people long gone, archaeology has created several theoretical ideas that are of value to all who study material culture.

Context

Objects do not exist in a void. The Grecian urn sitting inside a glass case in an urban museum can only tell us so much about how that object was viewed by the people who used it. It has been taken out of its original context. Was it originally made by a craftsman for a wealthy Greek businessman to sit on a prominent shelf boasting of its owner's wealth? Was it a functional piece, used to serve wine every night at dinner? Or was it carefully buried in a tomb as an offering to the gods to care for a deceased beloved? Without knowing how it functioned in its original context, the material culture analyst is at a loss to understand it. For archaeologists, the context is all important, as it leads us to an understanding as to how an object was used by the people who possessed it. In archaeology, this context is best understood by analyzing each object in the context of other objects found with it in a careful excavation. But examining the relationship between objects found together can also help those studying modern material culture.

The *Chaîne Opératoire*

Another way archaeologists try to understand artifacts is by attempting to trace how they were made. In contemporary culture, we are likely to accept an object in its finished form when we look to interpret it. This is changing as people look at the components of the global commodity chain (see chapter 13). But archaeologists have always had this concern. French archaeologist Andre Leroi-Gourhan developed the concept of *chaîne opératoire* in his 1964 book, *Le Geste et la Parole* (which translates, roughly speaking, as "gesture and speech"). The term *chaîne opératoire* means "operational chain" or "operational sequences," and refers to the attempt to reconstruct the way artifacts were manufactured and used and, in addition, to understand the place technical activities played in older human societies.

In *Le Geste et la Parole* Leroi-Gourhan wrote (1964:1640) that "techniques involve both gestures and tools, organized in a chain by a veritable syntax that simultaneously grants to the operational series their fixity and their flexibility." By this he meant that using his approach one should examine the relationship that exists between the technology needed to create an artifact and the role technologies play in societies. All artifacts involve decisions made by those who made them.

As Nathan Schlanger writes in his chapter on *The Chaîne Opératoire* in *Archaeology: The Key Concepts* (2005:29):

> In sum, much more than a method for reconstructing past techniques, the *chaîne opératoire* approach can lead from the static remains recovered in the present to the dynamic processes of the past, and thus open up a range of inspiring archaeological questions. With the *chaîne opératoire*, it is possible to appreciate that alongside tools, raw materials, energy and various physical

and environmental possibilities, technical systems are also
composed of such crucial elements as the knowledge, skills, values
and symbolic representation brought to bear and generated in
the course of action, as well as the social frameworks (including
gender, age or ethnic differentiation) implicated in the production
and reproduction of everyday life.

Leroi-Gourhan's approach realized that technology is a social activity, and thus archaeology must consider the social and cultural roots
and the entire web of actions that generated artifacts. While chaine
operatoire explains the context in which a tool is made and used, that
is not the end of its "life history."

Behavioral or Transformational Archaeology

In a chapter on "Archaeological Formation Processes" in *Archaeology: The Key Concepts,* Vincent M. Lamotta and Michael B. Schiffer offer us an overview of behavioral archaeology. They write (2005):

> Archaeologists learn about the human societies of the past by studying debris that has survived into the present. However, these material remains have not come down to us unchanged. In fact, virtually all of the "objects" that archaeologists study—artefacts, plant and animal remains, and architectural spaces—have been altered in significant ways by archaeological formation processes (also known as site formation processes). This term refers to all of the behavioural, mechanical and chemical processes that have modified an object from the time it was first made or used by people until its remains are recovered and studied.

This is an important point, for it calls our attention to the fact that most of the time the artifacts that archaeologists find and study have been considerably modified by either natural or cultural processes after their original manufacture, use, and discard.

Schiffer believes that archaeology should deal with the relationships that exist between human behavior and material culture during all periods and everywhere. Gamble's *Archaeology: The Key Concepts* describes Schiffer's approach as follows (2005:70):

> Michael Schiffer, once a Binford student, developed an approach that privileged the study of human behaviour—especially making, using and discarding artefacts. Schiffer...was interested in making explicit the multiple role of laws in archaeological research. For Schiffer it was not middle-range theory as much as the study of how the archaeological record was formed. These formation processes were of two types: natural and cultural. "N" and "C" transforms affected objects and their associations in predictable ways as they moved from the past, systemic context into the present archaeological context, where they become refuse.

This means that archaeology, for Schiffer, doesn't limit itself to studying ancient societies but is interested in how objects transform over time from the point of discard to the present. Did a broken piece of that Grecian urn serve as a spoon for a street urchin hundreds of years later? Was it washed downstream one rainy winter? Was it used to plug a hole in a wall or help fill the foundation for a later Greek Orthodox church?

These principles can be used in understanding modern objects as well. Tracing the history of an object from its creation through its various owners, uses, and modifications can tell us much about both the object and the people who used it.

Even garbage plays an important role in helping us understand past culture and gain important insights into contemporary ones, as well. For example, William Rathje of the University of Arizona conducted the "Garbage Project" in the 1970s and 1980s, excavating modern landfills to discover what we eat, what we discard, and how to minimize solid waste. Among his findings based upon discoveries in people's garbage cans: people lie in surveys about the amount of alcohol they drink.

Cognitive Archaeology

Even with the limitations of archaeological understanding of past objects, recent attempts have been made to understand the minds of prehistoric people. According to Colin Renfrew, cognitive archaeology involves inferring the way people thought in earlier times by studying material culture that survives from those times. It is not an attempt to understand the meaning these objects had for those who made them but, as he writes (2005:41), "the evident requirement is to develop a secure methodology by which we can hope to learn how the minds of the ancient communities in question worked, and the manner in which that working shaped their actions."

In their book, *The Ancient Mind: Elements of Cognitive Archaeology*, editors Colin Renfrew and Ezra B. W. Zubrow write (1994:3):

Cognitive archaeology—the study of past ways of thought as inferred from material remains—still presents so many challenges to the practitioner that it seems if not a novel, at any rate an uncertain endeavor. That this should be so is perhaps rather odd, for generations of archaeologists have written with considerable freedom about the thoughts and beliefs of ancient peoples, about the religions of early civilizations and about the art of prehistoric communities. With the New Archaeology of the 1960s and 1970s, however, came an acute awareness that much earlier work was in some respects not well founded, or at least that the frameworks of inference by which statements were made about past symbolic systems were rarely made explicit and were frequently defective.

Cognitive archaeologists, for Renfrew, are interested in the way humans use symbols and in the social relations that are needed for them to use symbols and communicate with one another. Students of modern material culture can use this and other inferential methods to better understand how to analyze contemporary objects.

Conclusions

We must recognize that every academic discipline has competing theories in it, each of which has different strengths and weaknesses. This explains why archaeologists, like scholars in many other areas, don't agree on which theories to hold and how to apply them. The theories to which we subscribe are important because they shape the way we conduct our research. Theories are like goggles we wear, and these goggles determine what we see and what we don't see.

Different kinds of archaeologists (and we can say the same for economists, sociologists, anthropologists, philosophers, and so on) wear different goggles and thus focus their attention on different things. And styles of goggles change, just like theories which become popular and then are often abandoned for newer ones that promise better ways of making sense of things. But, for archaeologists, who don't have the option of speaking with living people to do their research, these theories are derived from a careful examination of the details of objects, their context, production, use, distribution, and transformation after use. Thus their importance for those who wish to study material culture.

Part II
Applications

8.

Exchange

Kula Objects

Bronislaw Malinowski (1884–1942) was a Polish anthropologist who was involved in a research expedition to New Guinea and North Melanesia from 1914 to 1918. He learned the language of the islanders he was working with so he could speak to them in their native tongue and carefully observed their behavior.

Malinowski on the Kula

Malinowski discusses a remarkable ritual exchange phenomenon called the Kula in his book, *Argonauts of the Western Pacific,* a classic work of anthropological investigation. The Kula is an elaborate system involving the ritual exchange of two objects that travel in opposite directions among widely dispersed islands: a long necklace of red shells called *soulava,* and bracelets of white shells called *mwali.*

What Objects Mean, Second Edition by Arthur Asa Berger, 133–139.

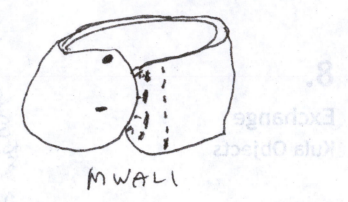

MWALI

Whenever the articles meet, Malinowski explains, they must be exchanged according to the rules and customs shaping the exchanges, and the articles then continue on their way, each in the proper direction. This exchange is based on detailed cultural codes that shaped the behavior of the participants. The objects were not bartered but were given as gifts that inevitably would lead to counter-gifts of the other kind of object. When they were exchanged, the participants offered detailed histories about who had owned them over the years. Every time an object moved it was regulated by a number of rules and conventions, and often by magic rituals and public ceremonies. The importance of the Kula is that objects, ideas, people, and relationships moved along with the necklaces and bracelets, and the formalized pattern of trading the Kula objects created opportunities for many other objects and information about them and about other matters to be transferred between islands.

The ritual exchange he discusses enmeshed the islanders in an enormously complex set of relationships. This ceremonial exchange, Malinowski reports, is the primary aim of the Kula, but there are secondary activities connected with it: magical rituals and public ceremonies. When you piece all the parts together you find that the Kula is an enormously complex institution, of which the participants were unaware. Those involved in the Kula knew what immediate roles they played when they came in contact with the shells or necklaces, but they were unaware of the Kula as an institution. Their actions had a significance for them, but they only saw a small part of the system and so weren't aware of it as a totality.

This leads Malinowski to suggest that ethnographers shouldn't dismiss as trivial various activities of the people they study that don't seem to be related to one another or don't seem of any consequence, but should look for rules that shape people's behavior and try to piece things together and get the big picture. The fact that the Trobriand islanders were involved in a gigantic institution whose contours and significance escaped them leads to an important insight: people do not necessarily understand the importance and significance of things they do and objects they own.

The Kula, Malinowski reported, was tied to myths, laws, and ceremonies, and there were complicated rules for every aspect of the exchange of necklaces and bracelets, objects that were of no practical use but had great symbolic value, and those involved in the Kula were tied to lifelong partnerships. Still, they didn't grasp the significance of the Kula in totality, in part because that kind of thought was beyond their capacities. We might wonder whether some of our activities can be seen as part of larger institutions that are like the Kula in that we do not recognize their nature—their covert and latent functions. It is often the case that observers from other countries or cultures notice things about our behavior that we do not see because we are so accustomed to the behavior that we cannot recognize its significance.

Malinowski discusses behavior analogous to the Kula in modern societies. He discusses a visit he paid to Edinburg Castle six years after his research when he was shown the Crown jewels. He writes (1922/1961:88):

> The keeper told many stories of how they were worn by this or that kind of queen on such and such occasion, how some of them had been taken over to London, to the great indignation of the whole Scottish nation, how they were restored, and how now everyone can be pleased, since they are safe under lock and key. As I was looking

at them and thinking how ugly, useless, ungainly, even tawdry they were, I had the feeling that something similar had been told to me of late, and that I had seen many other objects of this sort, which made a similar impression on me.

And then arose before me the vision of a native village on coral soil, and a small, rickety platform temporarily erected under a pandanus thatch, surrounded by a number of brown, naked men, and one of them showing me long, thin, red strings, and big, white, worn-out objects, clumsy to sight and greasy to touch. With reverence he also would name them, and tell their history, and by whom and when they were worn, and how they changed hands, and how their temporary possession was a great sign of the importance and glory of the village.

The crown jewels and the arm shells and necklaces that circulated in the Kula were both examples of objects being "possessed for the sake of possession itself," he writes, and we see in the Crown jewels and the objects involved in the Kula the same mindset at work and the same valuation because of their historical importance. The same kind of thing is at work in our valuation of antiques or furniture and other objects handed down over generations in our families. By owning them, even though they may be useless, we get increased status.

Malinowski also wrote about what he called "imponderabilia" of everyday life—our working routines, the foods that we eat, our conversations and social lives, the things we own and exchange for other things—that must to be studied to determine the values and beliefs reflected in them. He explains his notions about imponderabilia as follows (1961:18–19):

> Here belong such things as the routine of a man's working day, the details of his care of the body, of the manner of taking food and preparing it; the tone of conversational and social life around the village fires, the existence of strong friendships or hostilities... All these facts can and ought to be scientifically formulated and

recorded, but it is necessary that this be done, not by a superficial registration of details, as is usually done by untrained observers, but with an effort at penetrating the mental attitude expressed in them.

Thus, mere description is not enough, Malinowski says, for our ultimate aim at analyzing objects and artifacts is to discover the attitudes people have about the objects they own and to discern what they reflect about the culture and society in which they were created.

One facet of the Kula that relates to contemporary life involves the matter of reciprocity in gift exchanging. The natives involved in the Kula were bound by codes and conventions to give a gift of equal value to the one they received, though with the Kula the gift giving was circular in nature in that the gifts were always moving on after being held and treasured for an indefinite period of time. So everyone involved in the Kula acted on the basis of blind faith—though the codes of the Kula required that ceremonial gifts of equal status be exchanged everywhere.

The Law of Reciprocity and Gift Giving

The law of reciprocity is a central component of gift giving in most societies. From a sociological perspective, giving gifts is a means of initiating or maintaining social relationships; that is, gift giving has functions and requires of us a complex set of calculations. In an article, "The Christmas Gift Horse" (in A. A. Berger (ed.), *About Man: An Introduction to Anthropology*, 1974:82), Sheila Johnson draws upon French sociologist Marcel Mauss's 1925 book, *The Gift*, to explain gift giving. She writes:

Aside from the basic decision to give a gift, which in itself may involve some delicate calculations, there are several other questions that must be settled. How much should it cost? Too expensive, and the recipient may be embarrassed or feel obligated to go out and buy you something equally costly; too cheap, and he might feel insulted. What sort of object should it be? A gift reflects the giver's taste, but it can also reflect the impression the giver has formed of the recipient's taste, providing more room for intended or unintended results...

The cardinal rule of gift-giving that lies behind these calculations is the principle of reciprocity...Reciprocity is what keeps social relationship on a more or less equal and friendly footing. A person who does not, or cannot, reciprocate is either signaling that he wants to end a friendly relationship or he puts himself in a socially subordinate position to the person from whom he accepts unilateral gifts.

We see, then, that giving the "right" gift to a person requires a great deal of speculation and can be fraught with peril. That explains why we often give people gifts of food or alcoholic beverages, since these gifts pose fewer problems in terms of our calculating what the right gift should be for the person to whom we are giving the gift. And they can be exchanged easily. The pressure to give gifts, and to give people the right gifts, is particularly strong during the Christmas period in many Western countries and leads to a great deal of anxiety and stress (sometimes financial, as well) among Christians (and many non-Christians, as well) who are involved with obligatory gift giving.

When we look for the mental attitudes and ideas expressed in gifts and objects in general, Malinowski would suggest that we are study-ing material culture the proper way. But "penetrating" the mindset of people is not easy to do, for as Freud has explained, many of our feel-ings and attitudes about objects are buried deep in our unconscious, and we are unaware of them. The example offered earlier by Dich-ter, about cigarette lighters, is an example of this. We can often learn about the meaning of our artifacts and possessions by examining our dreams about them and interpreting the myths and rituals that shape our behavior in curious ways. And we can also examine print adver-tisements and television commercials, which function like dreams and play an important role in shaping the way we think about objects and in persuading us to purchase them.

Questions for Discussion and Topics for Further Research

1. Malinowski suggested that complex social structures are reflected in objects. Select an object in contemporary life and explain the complex social structure it reflects using the theories discussed in the first part of this book.

2. The Kula has been described as having no utilitarian purpose. Do you think that is correct? What functions other than utility might the Kula have? What behaviors do we engage in that have no utilitarian purpose? What behaviors do we engage in that are similar in nature to the Kula?

3. Which social sciences and theories does Malinowski use in his analysis?

4. What was said about reciprocity and gifts? Apply psychoanalytic theory and functional analysis to gift giving.

5. How might a Marxist interpret the Kula? What elements in the Kula would be of particular interest to Marxist theorists?

9.
Style
Blue Jeans

Semioticians would say that the clothes we wear can be seen as "messages" to others about ourselves. We are always sending messages to others, through our clothing, our body language, our facial expressions and just about everything else we do. Sometimes, psychoanalytic critics would suggest, we don't realize the full extent of the messages about ourselves that we are sending. So blue jeans are full of messages, and decoding these messages for what they reveal about socio-economic class, attitudes towards authority, and sexuality is not easy.

I once decided to count the number of my students in one of my classes who were wearing blue jeans. It turned out that every student in the class that day was in blue jeans.

What Objects Mean, Second Edition by Arthur Asa Berger, 141–149. © 2014 Taylor & Francis. All rights reserved.

One of the most intense fashion wars that's currently taking place in the United States (and in other parts of the world) isn't between lower-class and elite fashions but between rival brands of blue jeans. Levi's, which at one time dominated the blue jeans field, has not done well for a number of years, as it battles with rival brands of blue jeans, such as Diesel, that are seen as more fashionable and stylish and have become more popular. They are also more expensive.

Human history, we can say, began with our wearing clothes. When God discovered that Adam and Eve were covering up their nakedness, it indicated to Him that they had disobeyed Him and eaten from the tree of knowledge, and they were then expelled from the Garden of Eden. It is possible to see wearing clothes as being connected to mythic thinking. Myths can be defined as sacred narratives that have an important role in shaping human behavior. I have already discussed what I call a myth model that connects myths to historical events, to reflections in elite and popular culture, and to everyday life. The myth model that deals with fashion and clothing is shown below:

Myth	Adam and Eve in the Garden of Eden
Psychoanalytic Theory	Nudism as expression of innocence
Historical Reflection	Pioneers in buckskins
Elite Arts	Gogol's "The Overcoat"
Popular Culture	Power dressing guides and books
Everyday Life	Wearing a pair of blue jeans

Although deciding to wear a pair of jeans is a personal decision, the myth model suggests that it may be connected, in our personal and cultural unconscious, to myths that shape our behavior in ways we do not recognize.

Marxists also have interesting things to say about blue jeans. In his book, *Commodity Aesthetics, Ideology & Culture* (1987:157–158), Wolfgang Haug, a German Marxist, offers some insights into the economic and complicated and contested cultural significance of blue jeans. Wearing jeans began, he says, in youth culture in bourgeois societies but then spread far beyond it, eventually invading socialist countries. He explains that blue jeans have a dual valence: they function both as a reflection of insubordination by the young—that is, a rejection of formal dress codes—and as an object of mass culture.

Jeans are, he asserts, a sign of protest against bourgeois "stuffed-shirt" gentlemen's fashion and everything that goes with bourgeois culture. In recent years, interestingly enough, jeans culture has gone up-market, and there are boutiques where jeans costs hundreds of dollars, much more than a bourgeois pair of slacks or a pair of woman's pants. But for the most part, jeans—as exemplars of leisure couture—stand at the opposite pole of what we might describe as "high fashion."

These differences between jeans and high fashion are shown below, though with the development of upscale high-end jeans, the differences aren't as strong as they originally were:

Blue Jeans	High Fashion
common material (denim)	fancy materials
cheap	expensive
work	leisure
uniformity	individuality
mass produced	hand made
department store	boutique

The widespread popularity of denim suggests that the distinction between work and play is diminishing, since people often wear denim, a "leisure" fabric, to work. Sociologists would tell us that denim also enables people to hide their socio-economic status, so it enables people to play with their identities.

Haug discusses a jeans advertisement that attracted his attention and reflects his concerns about the way advertisers use sexuality to sell jeans. He writes:

> In the struggles for competence in fashion the jeans-side is by no means one-upped by the conservative offense. The advertisement for one jeans store is exemplary in this regard. The photo shows us that now-familiar portion of the body, the hind side, this time nude and female. From its forms the emblem of the firm is likewise constructed. Text: We are jeanspros and we fight against stuffed-shirt-fashions. For a free life, active and fresh, that is fun and doesn't give the vampires of constraint a chance....
>
> "Protest fashion" has its origin and dynamics in the "horizontal" elements of socialization, i.e., in the beginnings of an anti-ideological culture-of-the-masses themselves. Its opposite is not correctly grasped in the category of "stuffed-shirt-fashion." It is, rather, the gentlemen's fashion, in which the subjects of bourgeois class domination appear.

Haug suggests that the opposing style for jeans is not what stuffed shirts wear but gentlemen's fashion, which suggests something involving old money and class.

From a Marxist perspective, jeans, perhaps more than any other kind of clothing, play a role in shaping false consciousness. They mystify the masses and help convince them that we are all living in classless, all middle class societies where everyone, even those living in so-called "pockets of poverty," has access to blue jeans. We find billionaires, who use jeans to hide their wealth and status, and homeless people wearing blue jeans.

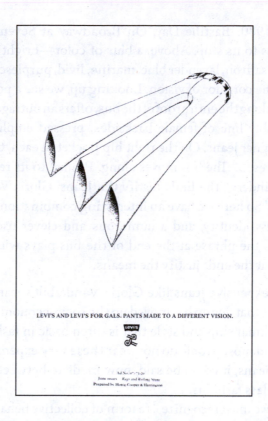

LEVI'S AND LEVI'S FOR GALS. PANTS MADE TO A DIFFERENT VISION.

In his book, *Radical Chic,* Tom Wolfe describes the difference in styles between members at the two ends of the socio-economic spectrum. He writes about socialite women at a party in "bell-bottom silk pants suits, Pucci clings, Gucci shoes [and] Capucci scarves," and contrasts them with some Mexican field workers "all in work clothes, Levi's chinos, Sears balloon seat twills, K-Mart sports shirts." When not at their fancy parties, these socialites might wear blue jeans—but probably designer jeans and not Levi's or other mass produced jeans.

In their book, *Channels of Desire: Mass Images and the Shaping of American Consciousness,* Stuart and Elizabeth Ewen discuss an interesting advertisement for blue jeans that they saw on a bus in New York. They write (1982):

July 14, 1980: Bastille Day. On Broadway at Seventy-second, a bus rattles to its stop. Above, a blur of color—bright red, orange, shocking saffron, lavender blue, marine, livid, purplescent, raven— invades the corridor of vision. Looking up, we see a poster ad that, running along the entire roof of the bus, offers an outrageous display: an assembly line of female backsides, pressed emphatically into their designer jeans. On the right hip pocket of each, the signature of an heiress... The bus moves along. Pinned to its rear we see its final reminder: "The Ends Justify the Jeans. Gloria Vanderbilt for Murjani." So here we have an interesting combination of sexuality, upper-class identity, and a humorous and clever use of Marxist theory, as the phrase at the end of the bus plays with Marxism's notion that the ends justify the means.

The rise of expensive jeans like Gloria Vanderbilt's jeans and many others shows that denim has moved up the socio-economic ladder, but it is the workmanship and style that is often basic in fashion, not the material. And most people do not wear these very expensive designer jeans. Blue jeans, it could be said, now mediate between lower-class and upper-class fashions.

Fashion, we must recognize, is a form of collective behavior, so when people in large numbers adopt blue jeans, they are following the dic-tates—or more precisely, the hidden imperatives—of fashion. As Rene Koenig writes in *The Restless Image: A Sociology of Fashion* (1973:51):

Fashion is indeed an unacknowledged world power. Even in the great clamor of world history, it guides man with a soft yet insistent voice. But again and again we feel its all-pervading presence and stare transfixed at the great public figures of the day who sometimes have themselves been carried to the top by the currents of fashion. Fashion is thus perhaps more powerful than all the other powers of the earth.

Koenig might have made his case a bit strongly, but there is no question that fashion, as a form of collective behavior, has a direct impact on people everywhere.

Koenig reminds us that fashion is a form of collective behavior, and many of the choices people make about fashion involve going along with fads, with what other people are wearing, with what movie stars, celebrities, and sports heroes wear or tell us to wear, in ads and commercials. Teenagers are under constant peer pressure to wear "in" styles, and many of them find themselves forced to go along with the latest trends in order to avoid standing out or being labeled "uncool."

Orrin E. Klapp, a sociologist, suggests in his book, *Collective Search for Identity*, that fashion is important for people who have something to prove about themselves. He makes a distinction between "front," which is fashion that reinforces one's status and identity, "fad," which is an experiment in identity, and "pose," which involves using fashion to claim status, education, and attainments to which one is not entitled. He believes that an important change has taken place in fashion and writes (1962:109):

> Fashion has always advertised the person and "costumed the ego," as Edward Sapir said; but the tendency to extremes (ego screaming) and garishness and bad taste today suggest that it is doing more along these lines and less for its traditional function of class maintenance. Fashion is ceasing to be a hallmark by which classes can distinguish themselves and more a highly theatrical venture in identity.

He wrote this book in the sixties. Since then, wearing blue jeans, or what I call "denimization," has become a means for everyone to hide their social class and status and to confuse others about gender. The blue jeans phenomenon is also part of a fashion revolution that has taken place in the United States, where, since the late sixties, women's clothing stores report now that they sell more pants than skirts. Charles Winick, a sociologist who wrote a book, *Desexualization in American Life*, arguing that contemporary American men are being feminized, would suggest that this represents a subtle kind of desexualization going on in America, as women have now started dressing in fashions previously reserved for men. As he explains (1995:229), "No important style has ever been adopted because of its practicality, and trousers are no exception. They have been becoming tighter, more tapered, and less comfortable than the looser styles of previous years." The fact that women are wearing so many blue jeans suggests that something other than practicality is behind the practice. The cuts of many brands of women's jeans are designed to emphasize their rear ends and thus are also a form of sexual display. Blue jeans are pants and thus were associated for many years with men, but are now used, thanks to cuts that emphasize the rear ends of women who wear them, as a means of being sexually attractive.

Blue jeans, we see, are a rather complicated kind of object, subject to many different forms of analysis. They are of interest to semioticians, since they can be seen as "messages" we send to others about ourselves—messages that may convey many different things. For Marxists, they reflect the power of youth culture and the breakdown of the distinction between work and leisure, since many people now wear jeans—defined as leisure wear—to work. For sociologists, jeans are part of fashion, a form of collective behavior, that have a number of different functions. One sociologist, Charles Winick, sees the popularity of jeans as an example of desexualization—now both men and women wear pants much of the time—going on in American society. And I have suggested that jeans may be connected to certain myths functioning in American society and culture.

So jeans are objects of considerable interest and fascination to scholars from a variety of disciplines, each of whom has different insights to offer in regard to jeans' cultural significance.

Questions for Discussion and Topics for Further Research

1. What brands of blue jeans do you own or have you owned? What's the difference between them? What are the most popular brands now? Use the theories we have discussed to explain why they are so popular.

2. How would you define "youth culture"? Do you think its influence has grown or diminished in recent years?

3. Are jeans an example of desexualization? Something else? Explain your answer.

4. Jeans can be analyzed from a number of different perspectives, such as semiotics, Marxism, psychoanalytic, and sociological. Which of these perspectives offers the most valuable insights into the jeans phenomenon? How would theorists from each of the perspectives just mentioned analyze the blue jean phenomenon?

5. What culture-codes are connected to wearing blue jeans? What would be the American code (using Rapaille's theories) for the blue jean?

10.

Technology

Smartphones

The astounding popularity of the smartphone is evident in our daily lives. A smartphone is defined as follows:

> a cellular telephone with built-in applications and Internet access. In addition to digital voice service, modern smartphones provide text messaging, e-mail, Web browsing, still and video cameras, MP3 player and video playback and calling. In addition to their built-in functions, smartphones run myriad free and paid applications, turning the once single-minded cellphone into a mobile personal computer.

> (www.pcmag.com/encyclopedia/term/51537/smartphone)

It is not unusual to see smartphones in use—by everyone from junior high school students to senior citizens everywhere and anywhere.

What Objects Mean, Second Edition by Arthur Asa Berger, 151–159. © 2014 Taylor & Francis. All rights reserved.

Pew Reports points out that smartphones play an important role in our daily lives, and for many Americans, they are the primary way they access the Internet nowadays (pewinternet.org/Reports/2013/Cell-Internet.aspx). There are approximately 6.8 billion cell phones in use now, which means, since the world population is around seven billion people, there is approximately one smartphone or cell phone for everyone in the world. And in some countries, such as the UK, Italy, and Sweden, cell phone and smartphone penetration is greater than 100 percent, which means just about everyone capable of using a cell phone or smartphone has one, and some people have more than one phone. As technology evolves, more people are buying smartphones to replace their less evolved cell phones.

For many people it would seem that these phones are often used to assuage a kind of loneliness they feel, and using them can be seen as an attempt to deal with a feeling of alienation and a sense of isolation—a consequence, some would say, of the modern world and technology that both empower us and, at the same time, alienate us. Marxists would say these feelings are a result of the bourgeois society we all live in that generates this alienation in everyone. Freudians would say that smartphone use is a reflection of our unconscious needs for affiliation and for affection and plays a role in our development of an identity.

Erik Erikson, a psychoanalyst, has a theory about human development that can be used to help us understand the role that smartphones play in our lives. In his book, *Childhood and Society* (1963), he offers a theory about the eight crises we all face, at different stages in our lives, as we grow older. I have not dealt with the two crises we face in infancy, since at those stages we don't use smartphones. I list Erikson's crises, which all take the form of polar oppositions, and then suggest the functions that smartphones play relative to these crises. The material on the eight crises is found in his chapter, "The Eight Ages of Man."

Stage	Crisis	Smartphone Functions
Childhood	Initiative/Guilt	Family Integration, Play, Amusement
School	Industry/Inferiority	Socialization, Schoolwork Skills
Adolescence	Identity/Role Confusion	Peer Group Bonding, Schoolwork, Romance
Young Adult	Intimacy/Isolation	Love, Career Initiation
Adult	Generativity/Stagnation	Career, Community
Maturity	Ego Integrity/Despair	Contact, Community

Erikson argues that as we grow up, we all face these crises and have to figure out a way to deal with them successfully as we move from infancy to old age. His analysis of adolescence and its crisis of "Identity and Role Confusion" is helpful in understanding smartphone use by young people. Adolescents, he argues, are disturbed by the problems they face relative to finding an occupation and, at that stage, tend to over-identify with heroes and celebrities of one kind or another. As he writes (1963:261):

> To a considerable extent adolescent love is an attempt to arrive at a definition of one's identity by projecting one's diffused ego image on another and by seeing it thus reflected and gradually clarified. This is why so much of young love is conversation.

This helps explain countless text messages young people send one another. These messages are significant because they play an important role in attempts at self-definition by adolescents. The table that follows shows how many teens have smartphones and tablets. In just one year, we find, the percentage of male and female teens and preteens with smartphones has increased a great deal.

**US Teenager Smartphone and Tablet Use 2012 and 2013
(Who Own or Have Access to a Device)**

Male Smartphone 2012	Male Smartphone 2013	Female Smartphone 2012	Female Smartphone 2013
44%	67%	42%	61%

Male Tablet 2012	Male Tablet 2013	Female Tablet 2012	Female Tablet 2013
43%	68%	47%	67%

In a fascinating column in the *New York Times*, "Lord of the Memes," David Brooks deals with changes that have taken place in what might be called "intellectual affectation" (August 8, 2008:A19). There have been, he suggests, three epochs of importance. The first, from 1400 to 1965, was one of snobbery, in which there was a hierarchy of cultural artifacts with works from the fine arts and opera at the highest level and the strip tease at the lowest level. In the 1960s, he writes, high modernism was in vogue.

In the late 1960s this epoch was replaced by what he calls the "Higher Eclectica." This epoch was characterized by dumping the arts valued in the epoch of snobbery in favor of a mixture of arts created by members of "colonially oppressed out-groups." What he is describing, though he doesn't mention it, is the impact of postmodernism upon culture, with its emphasis on eclecticism and the pastiche. It was "cool" to have a record collection with all kinds of "world" music and to decorate your house with religious icons or totems from Africa or Thailand.

"But on or about June 29, 2007, human character changed," Brooks writes. "That, of course, was the release date of the first iPhone. On that date, media displaced culture." What that means is that the way we transmit things, media, replaced the content of what we create, culture. Really hip and cool people can be recognized as such because they are both early adopters and early discarders of the newest gizmos. Brooks was writing a satirical article, but his notion that American culture really changed when the iPhone was introduced isn't too far-fetched. Having a cell phone was of use to many supporters of the Democratic presidential nominee Barack Obama, for he indicated his choice of a vice president by sending text messages and e-mail messages to people who had registered their phones and e-mail addresses with him before he announced his choice to the press.

Two scholars, Louis Leung and Ran Wei, offer a sociological perspective on cell phone use in their article, "More Than Just Talk on the Move: Uses and Gratifications of the Cellular Phone," which appeared in the *Journalism and Mass Communication Quarterly* (Summer, 2000:2). They explain that cell phones provide such things as mobility and immediacy (that is, immediate access to others) to cell phone users, and they also allow users to show affection by enabling us to connect to friends and family members. This approach focuses upon the social uses and psychological gratifications provided by cell phone communication to people using these devices.

Smartphones are popular because they are so useful in so many different ways. For example, teenagers like them because they escape from surveillance of their calls by their parents. These phones play a role, then, in what psychologists call the separation and individuation process. Parents often give cell phones or smartphones to their children in order to keep tabs on them and maintain contact with them wherever they are. The phones can function, we see, as a kind of electronic leash.

There are negative aspects to the widespread use of smartphones and cell phones in general. They can be a big public nuisance, since many people with smartphones have conversations in public places, often with a loud voice, where they disturb others near them. Soon American airlines may be allowed to enable passengers to use their phones during flights, which has generated a great deal of controversy. The idea of spending hours sitting next to a person chatting on a cell phone is not appealing to most people. It has been found that people talking on the phone or texting while driving have, on a percentage basis, a large number of accidents, and many states now ban drivers from talking on cell phones and require them to use headsets or other hands-free devices. Most states ban texting while driving, and around a quarter of the states ban talking on the phone while driving.

Before the first iPhone was released, there was a widespread hysteria among Apple fans, and some people actually camped out on sidewalks in front of Apple Stores so they could be sure they would get one. Each year since has seen the release of a newer, more powerful iPhone with expanded features, along with a variety of competing options from manufacturers such as Samsung, Motorola, HTC, LG, and Nokia. And yet the iPhone has been an enormous success and has become a cultural icon.

The question arises—why do people feel it necessary to spend so much time on smartphones and cell phones? Do people use them to make calls they need to make or use them because they have them at their disposal and want to use them because they are lonely and feel the desire to speak with someone—maybe anyone? For some people, these phones free them from having to stay in offices to conduct business. They can work out at a gym or go for a run and still be available to reach others who may need to talk with them. These phones (along with blue jeans) seem to have blurred the distinction between work and play since, thanks to these phones, it is possible to do both. These phones have also blurred the difference between private and public, with many people conducting conversations in public places with loud voices—disturbing others and forcing them to imagine what is being said by the person on the other end of the call.

It may be that people are so pressed for time nowadays that they have to multi-task, so using cell phones becomes an indicator of a level of widespread cultural stress. Marxists might see cell phone use as an example of the alienation and loneliness people feel in bourgeois capitalist countries, where people are pitted against one another and are susceptible to advertisements and social pressures that convince them they must own smartphones. These phones also have revolutionary aspects, enabling people in third world countries to skip the land phone stage of telephony, and the PC stage of internet connectivity.

In an article titled "Smartphone Upgrades Slow as the 'Wow' Factor Fades" by Spencer E. Ante in the *Wall Street Journal* (July 17, 2013:B1) he suggests that our fascination with new smartphones may be fading a bit. Ante points out that since we now have 70 percent of contract subscribers with smartphones, there are fewer people available to upgrade to smartphone usage and data plans, and the changes to smartphones have been relatively modest, so users are not as tempted to upgrade as frequently as they did in years past. Thus, many smartphone users stick with the phones they've been using for the past two or three years while they wait for "the next big thing" in smartphones to be created.

In addition, some plans now allow smartphone users to change their phones whenever they want, without penalties, instead of having to wait for two years.

It is interesting to note that when Apple introduced two iPhones in September, 2013 (an upgrade for one and an inexpensive plastic covered version of the old iPhone), it sold nine million phones in one week. So our passion for iPhones and other smartphones continues, even though it may not be as feverish as it was in recent years.

Questions for Discussion and Topics for Further Research

1. Do we all use smartphones the same way, or are they used in different ways by different groups (age, gender, etc.) in different countries?

2. How have smartphones evolved over the years? What new developments are being considered?

3. How do the various theories discussed in the book help us explain the economic, psychological, social, and cultural significance of smartphones? How would Sigmund Freud, Karl Marx, Roland Barthes, Clotaire Rapaille, Mary Douglas, and Lewis Binford analyze the smartphone phenomenon?

4. What did Erikson say about teenagers that helps us understand their smartphone use?

5. What unconscious factors might make people feel they need smartphones and need to keep changing them every year or so?

6. Answer these questions posed by Howard Rheingold in *Smart Mobs* and discuss the impact of smart phones on specific objects and industries:

   How will human behavior shift when the appliances we hold in our hands, carry in our pockets, or wear in our clothing become supercomputers that talk to each other through a wireless mega-Internet? What can we reasonably expect people to do when they get their hands on the new gadgets? Can anyone foresee which companies will drive change and detect which businesses will be transformed or rendered obsolete by it? (Rheingold, 2003: xv–xvi)

11.

Globalization
Coca-Cola

If one were asked to fill a time capsule with the most important artifacts of the twentieth century, it would seem likely that a bottle of Coca-Cola would be included among the artifacts selected. Coca-Cola was invented in 1886 by a pharmacist in Atlanta, John S. Pemberton, and was first bottled in 1894. In 1902, Coca-Cola was incorporated. In 1915, Coke adopted the "classic" contour bottle, to differentiate itself from other drinks. The original glass bottle was an object that everyone could recognize during the years when glass bottles were being used and changed very little over the years. The bottle's cultural significance is reflected in the fact that it has often been painted by pop artists, such as Andy Warhol, who painted a large canvas in 1962 with 210 Coke bottles.

What Objects Mean, Second Edition by Arthur Asa Berger, 161–169.

Coca-Cola is what I would describe as a diluted narcotic (being vaguely related to cocaine), and for many people it is seen as a way they can reward themselves with a "luxury" item at little expense. Diet Coke provides a means of obtaining pleasure without consequences (gaining weight), which suggests that it can be seen as a repudiation of the cultural Puritanism that has so long shaped American character and culture. Curiously, in its original formulation, Coca-Cola was sold as a patent medicine. So it has evolved from a medicine to the world's most popular non-alcoholic beverage, sold in 200 different countries.

In an essay that appeared in Marshall Fishwick and Ray B. Browne's *Icons of Popular Culture* (1970), Craig Gilborn wrote an essay, "Pop Iconology: Looking at the Coke Bottle," suggesting that Coca-Cola is "the most widely recognized commercial product in the world" (1970:24). He quotes a statistic about a study made in 1949 that showed that only one person out of 400 could not identify by the bottle what product was being sold. This was before the rise of McDonald's and Starbucks, but I believe that Gilborn's contention is still correct about Coca-Cola's global reach.

Now that it is sold in cans, Coca-Cola doesn't have as good a way to differentiate itself, physically, from other kinds of soda pop, though it does have its distinctive colors and the Coke typography. Coca-Cola is a universally recognized signifier of American culture and society, and drinking cokes was a way for people, all over the world, to indicate their sense of attachment to the United States and to modernity.

This point was made by folklorist and anthropologist Raphael Patai in his book, *Myth and Modern Man*. He explains the role advertising has in our pleasure in drinking Cokes. He writes (1972:238–239):

It has been observed by critics of the American mass media that the method used in television commercials "never [to] present an ordered, sequential, rational argument but simply [to] present the product associated with desirable things, or attitudes." Thus Coca-Cola is shown held by a beautiful blonde, who sits in a Cadillac, surrounded by bronze, muscular admirers, with the sun shining overhead. By repetition, these elements become associated in our minds, into a pattern of sufficient cohesion, so that one element can magically evoke the others. If we think of ads as designed solely to sell the products, we miss their main effect: to increase the pleasure in the consumption of the product. Coca-Cola is far more than a cooling drink; the consumer participates, vicariously, in a much larger experience. In Africa, in Melanesia, to drink a Coke is to participate in the American way of life.

We are reminded here of Lefebvre's statement about the role advertising plays in consumer cultures, giving all the products people purchase their valuation. From a Marxist perspective, Coca-Cola and all soft drinks are examples of the way Capitalist societies create false needs in people, so they can be exploited. For Marxists, Coca-Cola becomes, like so many other aspects of American culture, a signifier of alienation and self-estrangement. It provides momentary gratification and distracts us from recognizing the degree to which we are exploited by the ruling classes.

Patai suggests that Coca-Cola also may be connected to mythological motifs about heroes who perform Herculean labors, so in partaking of Cokes we are associating ourselves, in an unconscious way, with the "Coke-drinking, laughing divinities" and sports heroes found in many Coca-Cola print advertisements and commercials. In a way, Coca-Cola may be seen as a functional equivalent of the magical ambrosias found in myths and folktales. For people who are no longer young, it reflects a form of magical thinking that enables them to identify with young people and delude themselves into thinking they are younger than they really are.

More than fifty years ago, in his book, *The Mechanical Bride: Folklore of Industrial Man*, McLuhan discussed the cultural significance of Coca-Cola (1951/1967:118, 120). He writes, analyzing the Coke ads of his time:

In *God Is My Copilot,* the G.I.'s agreed that what they were fight-ing for was, after all, the American girl. To us, they said, she meant cokes, hamburgers, and clean places to sleep. Now, the American girl as portrayed by the coke ads has always been an archetype. No matter how much thigh she may be demurely sporting, she is sweet, nonsexual, and immaturely innocent....

Margaret Mead's observations in *Male and Female* are especially relevant to understanding the success of coke ads. It is, she suggests, a result of our child-feeding habits that "Mouths are not a way of being with someone, but rather a way of meeting an impersonal environment. Mother is there to put things—bottles, spoons, crackers, teethers—into your mouth." And so, she adds, the American G.I. abroad puzzled foreigners by endless insistence of having something in his mouth most of the time. Gum, candy, cokes.

McLuhan's approach draws upon Freudian psychoanalytic theory, which suggests that all individuals pass through four stages as they develop: oral, anal, phallic, and genital. Coke, from his perspective, is connected to our oral stage and thus reflects a kind of momentary regression in adults drinking Coke. McLuhan was particularly interested in a cover for *Time* magazine that showed the globe sucking a coke—a signifier of its world-wide popularity.

One aspect of the Coca-Cola "contour" bottle that struck me is that its shape, especially the top half of the bottle, has a vague resemblance to a woman's breast, so the Coke bottle might have been connected to unconscious longings adults have to return to the blissfulness of infancy. This offers us another example of what would be described, in psychoanalytic terms, as a regression in the service of the ego—the same kind of regression we obtain when, as adults, we buy ice cream cones. Psychoanalytically speaking, it is a means of oral gratification. Its purchase is made possible by id desires for gratification overcom-ing ego restraints and superego guilt about spending money for Cokes instead of drinking water to slake one's thirst.

McLuhan also ties that popularity to "the American way" and American culture, suggesting that it was an artifact that suggested being modern and up-to-date. Coke also is connected, he adds, to notions Americans had about the wholesomeness of American life, and particularly of American women and American mothers:

> The coke has become a kind of rabbit's foot, as it were, for the foreigner. And *Time's* cover (May 15, 1950) pictures the globe sucking a coke. Love that coke, love that American way of life…Cokes as a soft drink naturally started out to appeal to the soft emotions. The wholesome harmlessness of the drink is insisted upon most successfully by the wholesome girls and situations which envelop the drink. These, in turn, have become linked to the entire range of home-mother-hygiene patterns which embrace a wide range of basic thoughts and feelings. So that it would be hard to suggest a more central item of current folklore, or one more subtly geared to evoke and release emotions of practical life today. Whether the drink was always as wholesome as the ads has been a matter of dispute among food analysts.

This question of Coke's "wholesomeness" has been settled by dietitians who point out that Coke and other soft drinks have around six teaspoons of sugar in each eight ounce serving.

Coca-Cola is connected in its advertising to youth culture and is a reflection, psychologist and anthropologist Clotaire Rapaille argues, of America being an adolescent culture. He argues in *The Culture Code* that because America never had royalty, it never had "to kill the king." We have always been rebellious, and our new immigrants pick up on this when they come to America. As he explains (2006:31):

> Our cultural adolescence informs our behavior in a wide variety of ways… Looking at our culture through this set of glasses explains why we are so successful around the world selling the trappings of adolescence: Coca-Cola, Nike shoes, fast food, blue jeans, and loud, violent movies.

Coca-Cola is, Rapaille argues, a reflection of America being an adolescent culture and can be seen, then, as a means for individuals, who may no longer be young, of identifying with youthfulness.

As the popularity of the United States has weakened in recent years, so has the popularity of Coca-Cola and its rival Pepsi Cola. Soda-pop of all kinds is losing popularity everywhere to bottled water and other beverages with less sugar and different tastes. Diet Coke, which uses artificial sweeteners, has hardly any calories, but many people complain that diet Coke and other diet drinks have a bitter after-taste. Coca-Cola, if you reduce it to its basic contents, is carbonated water with sugar and syrup with "secret" flavors.

What you get when you choose Coca-Cola, however, is the personality or the "aura" of the drink generated by the enormous amount of advertising by Coca-Cola. Walter Benjamin's theory about auras may explain the significance of Coke's campaign arguing that it is "the real thing." It is only the "real thing" that can generate an aura, so the argument for Coke is that if you want to partake of all the positive aspects of life associated with Coke, you have to drink Cokes and not Pepsi or other colas.

Blind taste tests show that most people cannot tell the difference between Coca-Cola and Pepsi Cola and generally prefer Pepsi. But when people are told that one glass has Coca-Cola and the other has Pepsi Cola, they tend to choose Coca-Cola as tasting better—in part because of the ubiquitous nature of Coke advertising and the cleverness of its advertising campaigns. Coca-Cola may be tied to the "American Way of Life," as McLuhan and Rapaille explain, but that brand, "the American Way of Life," has been losing its allure to many people in the United States and in other countries in recent years. That may help explain why sales for Coca-Cola and other cola drinks have been flat lately.

The Coca-Cola corporation induced Chinese basketball star Yao Ming to leave Pepsi and endorse Coca-Cola, a real coup in marketing terms. Coca-Cola had a huge presence in the 2008 Olympics in

China, and hoped to use its expensive campaign, estimated at around $400 million, to move ahead of Pepsi in the race to conquer the soft-drink market in China. According to a first page article in the *Wall Street Journal* titled "Coke Pins Hopes on Blitz in Beijing" (by Goeffrey A. Fowler and Betsy McKay, 2008), Pepsi is waging a campaign focusing on Chinese singers and Chinese youth culture. In 2007, the average person in China averaged only 35 eight ounce servings in a year, which is less than some Americans drink in a week. In America, the article points out, per capita soda consumption was 789 servings, which comes to more than two servings of soda a day. They write, "Coke is the global leader in the cola wars, with roughly half the market, more than double PepsiCo Inc.'s share."

In his book, *Ad Worlds,* Greg Myers, a linguistics professor from England, devotes a chapter to globalization and advertising. He discusses the famous Coca-Cola commercial from 1971 (1999:55):

> In 1971, the Coca-Cola Company produced a television commercial featuring 200 young people at sunrise on a hill, each dressed in some form of national dress, each holding a distinctive bottle of "Coke," and all singing along with the New Seekers:
>
> > *I'd like to buy the world a home and furnish it with love*
> > *Grow apple trees and honeybees and snow-white turtle doves*
> > *I'd like to teach the world to sing in perfect harmony*
> > *I'd like to buy the world a Coke and keep it company*
> > *It's the real thing.*
>
> We have found that people in focus groups still remember this ad a generation later. Dated as it may seem today, "Hilltop" set out a kind of ad that has since become ubiquitous. The Coca-Cola Company was one of the first companies to build its marketing strategy of a single global product and brand image. It was one of the first to use the globe itself, and the ethnic and national diversity of consumers, as a sign of the brand's universal desirablity and availability.

The catchy "Hilltop" song, Myers adds, with the Coke reference taken out, was issued as a single record and became Number One in the U.S. charts. He points out that many multi-national companies use global themes, but they also have to be aware of differences in each country and tailor their ads to take national character and regional differences into consideration.

An article on the "Hilltop" commercial by Robert Glancey spells out its meaning (quoted in Robert Goldman and Stephen Papson, *Sign Wars: The Cluttered Landscape of Advertising*, 1996:271):

> The idea behind the advertising is that we really are part of some global Village: we all want the same things, we all have access to them and we all respond to the same imagery. Coca-Cola sells itself as democratic, international and liberating; no wonder it's good for you.

In recent years, with the global epidemic of obesity, people everywhere are beginning to realize that Coke and other sugar-loaded soft drinks aren't healthy, and now there are big challenges from other kinds of beverages that Coca-Cola and its competitors face.

Questions for Discussion and Topics for Further Research

1. What does it mean when Coca-Cola says it's the "real" thing?

2. Find a Coke print advertisement and analyze it using the methodologies and theories discussed in the first part of this book. Which approach—semiotic, psychoanalytic, Marxist, sociological, or anthropological—was most interesting and most revelatory?

3. What points were made by McLuhan, Patai, and Rapaille in their analysis of Coke and Coke advertising?

4. How many cans (or servings) of soda-pop do you drink during a typical day? Which soda-pop brand do you like best? What does your brand choice say about you?

5. How would you respond to a Marxist critique of Coca-Cola that argues drinking it is an expression of self-alienation?

6. Are Coke drinkers fixated at what Freud called the oral level of development? Explain your answer using theories discussed in this book.

12.

Identity
Blonde Hair Dye

How do people obtain their identities? That's a question that social scientists, writers, philosophers and others have pondered over the millennia. For many people, identity is constructed of a combination involving race, religion, gender, body type, educational attainments, personality, and occupation. All of these considerations involve being a member of some group, some culture or subculture.

When we ask ourselves "Who am I?" the subtext of what we are asking is, many social scientists suggest, "To what group do I belong?" And when we know this, and locate ourselves in some group, we then know what rules we are to obey. Our identities affect

What Objects Mean, Second Edition by Arthur Asa Berger, 171–177. © 2014 Taylor & Francis. All rights reserved.

our behavior, because social roles are connected to our belonging to some group, to our status in the group, and to expectations people have of us due to our membership in the group. As we grow, we sometimes change our group affiliation, and this affects our identities and conduct.

One way people try to signify their identities is by their hair color. In Western consumer cultures, thanks to all the advertising to which we are exposed, we learn to think about hair color in certain ways. Many men and women believe that "blondes have more fun," and so they dye their hair blonde, believing that this color makes them seem younger, more stylish, and more modern. Blonde hair, we may say, not only helps confer an identity for people who are natural blondes but also for people who dye their hair blonde. Some aspects of fashion, such as hair color, not only help confer an identity on people but for a variety of reasons generate remarkably strong passions in those who have dyed their hair blonde—or any other color.

Roland Barthes, the distinguished French semiotician, discussed the importance of clothes and other objects in his book, *The Semiotic Challenge*. He writes (1988:147):

> A garment, an automobile, a dish of cooked food, a gesture, a film, a piece of music, an advertising image, a piece of furniture, a newspaper headline—these indeed appear to be heterogeneous objects.
>
> What might they have in common? This at least: all are signs. When I walk through the streets—or through life—and encounter these objects, I apply to all of them, if need be without realizing it, one and the same activity, which is that of a certain *reading*: modern man, urban man, spends his time reading. He reads, first of all and above all, images, gestures, behaviors: this car tells me the social status of its owner, this garment tells me quite precisely the degree of its wearer's conformism or eccentricity.

What Barthes is saying is that we are always, even when we are not conscious of doing so, "reading" or interpreting the messages sent by the things others say, do, and own; we are always interpreting messages sent by others, and they are interpreting the messages we send. One of the things we "read" about people, most immediately, is their hair style and hair color, each of which conveys certain messages about them.

Sometimes, of course, people "lie" with signs and drive cars above their socio-economic level or have hair colors that are not the hair colors they were born with. Barthes alerts us to the importance of deciphering social and cultural messages found in fashion and just about everything else we have and do. Some of these messages are global in nature.

One way we develop a personal identity is to identify with others we respect or idolize and imitate them in various ways. When it comes to our functioning as consumers, we often imitate the desire, as reflected in the advertisements they make, of celebrities, movie stars, and sports heroes who are blondes, either by nature or by desire. We must recognize that there are many different kinds of blondes, such as platinum blondes, strawberry blondes, dirty blondes, golden blondes, and peroxide blondes. So there are considerable variations in blondeness and many choices we have to make when choosing what kind of blonde to become when we dye our hair.

Sociologist Charles Winick offers some insights into the significance and functions of blonde hair in his book, *The New People: Desexualization in American Life.* He writes (1968:169):

Blonding requires a toner and bleach in a two-process treatment, even if the hair is naturally blonde. For some women, blonding is an opportunity to transcend their ethnic backgrounds. Others see it as a symbol of the child's light hair and towheadedness and for older woman, blonding is a simple way of covering gray. There are women who become blond because changing their hair is so profound an experience that they want a radically different hue. But for a substantial number of women, the attraction of blondeness is less an opportunity to have more fun than the communication of a withdrawal of emotion, a lack of passion. One reason for Marilyn

Monroe's enormous popularity was that she was less a tempestu-
ous temptress than a non-threatening child. The innocence con-
veyed by blonde hair is also suggested by the 70 percent of baby
dolls whose hair is blonde.

D. H. Lawrence pointed out that blonde women in American
novels are often cool and unobtainable, while the dark woman
represents passion. Fictional blondes also tend to be vindictive and
frigid....Over 20 percent of the sales of hair-coloring preparations
are for blonding although only 5 percent of American women have
the color naturally.

Winick wrote his book more than 40 years ago, and some of his
statistics are not correct, but his notion that blonde hair, unconsciously,
signifies a kind of withdrawal of emotion is worth considering. We
must ask—if a woman with black or brown or red hair dyes her hair
blonde, her hair color doesn't, we must assume, change her personality.
So women with dark hair colors who dye their hair blonde still have
the "passion" that D. H. Lawrence said they had, but their hair color
disguises this quality.

There are also stereotypes about blondes as "dumb" and many
jokes about dumb blondes. This stereotype is based on the notion that
blonde women use their beauty instead of their brains to get ahead in
the world. Anita Loos's novel, *Gentlemen Prefer Blondes,* reflects some
of these stereotypes about blondes. If we associate certain qualities
with blonde hair, then women who dye their hair blonde are, in a
sense, claiming an identity that is false; many a blonde "dyes by her
own hand," it has been said. And a large number of blondes are, we
can say, impostors who are lying with the blonde hair sign.

Orrin E. Klapp, a sociologist, quotes a wonderful advertisement
about blonde hair in his book, *Collective Search for Identity.* The ad
reads as follows (1969:78):

Maybe the real you is a blonde. Every smart woman keeps searching
for her identity—the inner woman she really is, and the outward

expression of it. She looks for a special way to shape her mouth or tilt her chin, a new color, a fragrance that is her personal message to the world. When you see a woman who has found herself, you know it. There's a quiet excitement about her that says "I like being me." Have you found the real you? Some women never do. In fact, many women never make the most exciting discovery of all: they should have been born blonde.

This advertisement suggests that dying one's hair represent a means of women finding their true identity—as blondes, and that the hair color they were born with actually prevents them from finding their identity. The logical implication of this advertisement is that every woman should be a blonde or, at least, many women should dye their hair and thus find their true identities. Klapp quoted this advertisement in his discussion of "looks," the way fashion in clothes and hair color enable people to have identity adventures.

An article on the amount of money and time women spend on their hair, which dealt with the topic in England, reveals women spend a great deal of money on their hair. An article by Deborah Dunham, posted on the internet on March 29, 2010, titled "The Price of Pretty: Women Spend $50,000 on Hair Over Lifetime" offers interesting statistics:

According to a British survey conducted by Tresemme, the average woman spends a staggering $50,000 on her hair over her lifetime. Each year, we spend an average of $160 on shampoos and conditioners, $120 for styling products and $520 for haircuts. And for those of us who color our locks, add in another $330 a year. But money is not the only significant investment we make in our quest for beauty. The amount of time we spend is also astounding when you add it up. We glamour girls spend an average of one hour and 53 minutes a week washing, blow drying and styling our hair. That may not sound like a lot, but by the time we reach the age of 65, we will have spent more than seven months of our lives on our hair!

We see, then, that hair care and coloring is really big business. One reason for this is because hair is the physical feature we have that is most easily modified and subject to our tastes and desires.

Sociologist Antony Synott has written an article, "Shame and Glory: A Sociology of Hair," in which he explains the role hair plays in our identities. He writes (September, 1989:381):

> Hair is perhaps the most powerful symbol of individual and group identity—powerful because it is physical and therefore extremely personal and second, although personal, it is also public rather than private. Furthermore, hair symbolism is usually voluntary rather than imposed or "given." Finally, hair is malleable, in various ways, and therefore singularly apt to symbolize both differentiations between, and changes in, individual and group identity.

We see, then, that hair color, as well as hair style (straight or curly, long or short, parted in the middle or on a side) is one of the most important signifiers available to us when we seek to confirm our identities. Synott quotes a figure of $2.5 billion spent on the hair industry in the United States in 1989—a figure he got from a *New York Times* article. A report in the *Economist* offers figures for global hair colorant sales, "The global market for hair colorants, already worth an annual $7 billion in retail sales, is expected to grow by 8–10% a year over the next five years. That makes it by far the fastest-expanding segment of the $37 billion hair-care industry" (www.economist.com/node/631692). That article appeared in 2001, which means the size of the hair-care industry now is much larger, being $49 billion in 2010 (www.reportlinker.com/ci02138/Hair-Care-Products).

So dying one's hair, either in a beauty parlor or at home, is a major industry and plays an important role in our everyday lives. The fact that we call places where women dye their hair and have their hair styled "beauty parlors" suggests that hair color and hair style play an incredibly important role in our lives and in the way we shape our identities.

Questions for Discussion and Topics for Further Research

1. Have you purchased any hair dye products because they were endorsed by a sports hero, movie star or celebrity? If so, why did you do so?

2. Why does hair color play such an important role in our psyches and our identities? What psychological and other benefits do people who dye their hair blonde get?

3. As Umberto Eco points out, signs can be used to mislead. Besides blonde hair dye, what are some other ways that people can lie with signs?

4. How might a Marxist analyze blonde hair dye? A semiotician? An archaeologist?

5. Are girls who dye their hair blonde because many celebrities and actresses have dyed their hair blonde examples of the diffusion of innovation? Explain your answer.

6. Using Freud's id, ego, and superego typology, place blondes, brunettes, and redheads in their correct categories. Justify your placements.

13.

Transformation
Books

Since 1450 and the invention of moveable type by Gutenberg, books have been available to large numbers of people. Books can be defined as manufactured objects with printed pages bound or hinged on one side. It is possible to purchase books with blank pages in art supply and stationery stores (I use this kind of book for my journals), but I am using the term in reference to books with printed matter in them. It is not only the ideas in books that are important but also the physical nature of books—the paper and the lines of printed matter that bring us these ideas as well as stories and pictures and many other things. This definition has been expanded in recent years with the growing popularity of eBooks—protected electronic text files which mimic the formatting of printed books and are readable on devices

What Objects Mean, Second Edition by Arthur Asa Berger, 179–188. © 2014 Taylor & Francis. All rights reserved.

such as smartphones, tablets, personal computers, and, especially, dedicated eBook readers such as Amazon's Kindle.

Reading a book involves reading letters that form words, and words that are, most of the time in the Western world, offered in horizontal lines of print that are read from left to right. It is possible to consider scrolls (such as the Torah), wall paintings, frescos, clay tablets, and manuscripts in other formats as books, but my focus will be on books as they are conventionally designed and manufactured in the Western world. Dedicated eBook readers can store hundreds of books on a reader and carry a whole library around on a very small device.

Books don't just suddenly appear, sprung from the head of Zeus. Somebody has to write a book. Once authors have had their manuscripts accepted by an acquisition editor, they find themselves dealing with development editors, who help them focus on important matters that might need more emphasis; production editors, who coordinate the design and production of the book; art editors and typographers, who are responsible for the way the book looks; copy editors, who go over the manuscript to make sure there are no typing, grammatical, or other kinds of errors in it; and proofreaders, who go over the page proofs to make sure there are no errors in them. Some authors who don't want to bother making indexes for their books hire professional indexers.

Books are composed of lines of print that are read in most countries from left to right. It is the linearity of print and the fact that individuals who read books and other kinds of printed texts can move through them at their own pace which fosters, Marshall McLuhan suggests, a number of different things, such as linear thinking, rationality, individualism, and a sense of detachment. You don't get these from electronic media, he argues. When you read a book you can skip back and forth in it, review what you've read any number of times, highlight certain passages with colored markers, and write comments in the margins about what you've read.

Marshall McLuhan (1911–1980), an influential Canadian media and culture theorist, explains his ideas about the social, cultural, and political impact of books in his classic work, *Understanding Media: The Extensions of Man* (1965:172–173):

Socially, the typographic extension of man brought in nationalism, industrialism, mass markets, and universal literacy and education. For print presented an image of repeatable precision that inspired totally new forms of extending social energies. Print released great psychic and social energies in the Renaissance, as today in Japan or Russia, by breaking the individual out of the traditional group while providing a model of how to add individual to individual in massive agglomeration of power. The same spirit of private enterprise that emboldened authors and artists to cultivate self-expression led other men to create giant corporations, both military and commercial.

Perhaps the most significant of the gifts of typography to man is that of detachment and noninvolvement...The fragmenting and analytic power of the printed word in our psychic lives gave us that "dissociation of sensibility" which in the arts and literature since Cezanne and since Baudelaire has been a top priority for elimination in every program of reform in taste and knowledge...It was precisely the power to separate thought and feeling, to be able to act without reacting, that split literate man out of the tribal world of close family bonds in private and social life.

What is important to recognize, McLuhan suggests, is that changes in the popularity of media have profound economic, political, social, and cultural consequences. And the development of new technologies, such as the cell phone or the computer and the internet, can have an enormous impact, whose ultimate dimensions we cannot appreciate or fathom at this time.

McLuhan was a literature professor who became interested in popular culture and media when he was looking for a way to reach his students. He found that advertising, the comics, and other media were useful ways of getting students to analyze literary texts and then, later, culture. As Donald Theall, a Canadian scholar, explains (*The Virtual Marshall McLuhan*):

> McLuhan became frustrated trying to teach first year students in required courses how to read English poetry, and began using the technique of analyzing the front page of newspapers, comic strips, ads, and the like as poems.... This new approach to the study of popular culture and popular art forms led to his first move towards new media and communication and resulted in his first book, *The Mechanical Bride*, which some consider to be one of the founding documents of early cultural studies. While the Bride was not initially a success, it introduced one aspect of McLuhan's basic method—using poetic methods of analysis in a quasi-poetic style to analyze popular cultural phenomena—in short, assuming such cultural productions to be another type of poem. (2001:4–5)

It was not a big step for McLuhan to start analyzing media in general, and that led to *Understanding Media* and a number of other books.

McLuhan distinguishes between hot media and cool media as follows (1965:22, 23):

There is a basic principle that distinguishes a hot medium like radio from a cool one like the telephone, or a hot medium like the movie from a cool one like TV. A hot medium is one that extends one single sense in "high definition." High definition is the state of being filled with data. A photograph is, visually, "high definition." A cartoon is low definition because very little visual information is provided....Hot media are, therefore, low in participation, and cool media are high in participation or completion by the audience.

McLuhan sees books as high definition since they make use of the phonetic alphabet and are loaded with information. Keeping in mind McLuhan's ideas about hot and cold media, we can consider the differences between electronic media and print media shown in the chart below, which is based on material found in *Understanding Media: The Extensions of Man.*

Electronic Media	Print Media
the ear	the eye
all-at-once	linearity
simultaneity	interconnectedness
emotion	logic
radio	books
community	individuality
involvement	detachment
pattern recognition	data classification

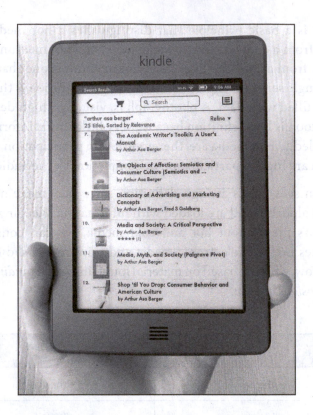

We might wonder whether developments in our new electronic media, such as the internet, Google, YouTube, and Facebook, will lead to changes in McLuhan's topics for electronic media, or whether what he wrote about radio and other media will still apply. McLuhan wrote about print media and electronic media; the eBook is a curious combination of a printed book that is electronically distributed. An eBook is an electronic version of a printed book. What would McLuhan have said about eBooks and the oppositions he made between print and electronic media? I would suggest that while eBooks are electronic, what they do is simulate print books, so eBooks can be seen as just a different way of transmitting print books.

McLuhan is famous for popularizing the notion of the global village and for arguing that "the medium is the message," which suggests that the impact of the media itself is more important than the content they carry. Many scholars repudiated McLuhan's notions when they first appeared, in part because of the jazzy style he used in writing and his interest in advertising and popular culture. But in recent years he has been re-evaluated, and many of his ideas are now widely accepted.

McLuhan's notions about the global village seem to have been borne out now that we have cell phones, YouTube, Facebook, My Space, Twitter, Google, e-mail, blogs, Skype, and other means of communication that link us all together into an electronic community or global village. Electronic media are becoming dominant now, and some print media, such as newspapers and magazines, are losing readers and struggling to survive.

In the contemporary world, characterized by McLuhan as being a global village, two books—the Bible and the Koran—and the religions based on them, are shaping our international and national politics. McLuhan's generalizations about print may help explain the "individuality" and sense of purpose that have led to a thousand years of terrible wars between different people who have different holy books. And these warring groups of people are now using electronic media, with incredible effectiveness, to spread their messages.

Books offer an interesting example of the way objects can be transformed, for books are now available in many different forms: printed books, audio books, and electronic devices such as the Amazon Kindle. There is also Google Books, which provides files of millions of books on the internet, and other sites that carry files of books. Audiobooks are also available, so people can listen to books being read to them as they commute to work, and they are now increasingly available on the web.

An article by Julie Bosman in the *New York Times* (May 15, 2013) offers statistics on the book industry. She reports on a survey by the book industry:

> The survey revealed that e-books now account for 20 percent of publishers' revenues, up from 15 percent in 2011. Publishers' net

revenues in 2012 were $15 billion, up from $14 billion in 2011, while unit sales of trade books increased 8 percent, to $2.3 billion.

It is very difficult to obtain reliable statistics on the book industry, but Bosman's report suggests that it is doing well, and eBooks are increasingly popular.

In his book *Counterblast*, published in 1969, McLuhan predicted, one might say, the evolution and transformation of the way books are made available to people in the electronic age. He wrote (1969:93), "Our obsession with the book as the archetype of culture has not even encouraged us to consider the book itself as a peculiar and arty way of packaging experience." Books, he added, are not becoming obsolete in the electronic age, but while books may have lost their pre-eminence as cultural artifacts, they have acquired new roles, and we might add, are acquiring new forms.

New technologies allow a publisher to print books "on demand," rather than printing a large number of them to take advantage of economies of scale. Print-on-demand technology allows publishers to avoid having to keep inventories of books, but each book is more expensive, so this technology is most useful for books that don't have large markets. In this digital age, anyone can become a publisher. There are electronic publishing sites, such as Amazon's CreateSpace, that writers can use to self-publish their books at minimal expense. There are other electronic book publishers, such as XLibris and IUni- verse, that provide more services, but they are much more expensive.

The problem with self-publishing books is that you have to mar- ket them yourself; generally speaking, self-published books don't sell many copies, but occasionally self-published books do find a market and some are republished by traditional publishers. So although book publishing has become democratized and anyone can be a publisher, the books we publish using print-on-demand internet publishers don't usually find a large market. In a typical year in the United States, we publish 100,000 books with traditional publishers and 200,000 books are self-published. Increasingly, more and more of these books are also published as eBooks.

As it becomes possible for more people to become authors, we must wonder whether the value of words is diminishing. When scribes hand copied manuscripts, word by word, every word had a certain value. That explains why Torah scrolls, each of which is hand copied by a scribe, are so valuable. Now, it seems that words have become cheapened and lost part of their importance.

The Roman writer Cicero (143–106 B.C.) wrote, "Times are bad. Children no longer obey their parents and everyone is writing books." With the development of internet publishers, everyone who is writing a book can now publish it at minimal expense. Whether anyone will purchase that book and read it is a different matter.

Questions for Discussion and Topics for Further Research

1. How does McLuhan derive individualism, detachment, and rationality from print? What other things does he say stemmed from print?

2. What are the differences, according to McLuhan, between electronic media and print media? What new developments have altered the relationship between electronic and print media? Explain your answer.

3. What theoretical approaches might explain the success of Amazon's Kindle and other eBook readers in recent years?

4. With the advent of self-publishing books with services such as Amazon's CreateSpace that publish books at little cost, has the landscape of published books changed for the better or the worse?

5. Do you agree that eBooks should be seen as print books in electronic form? What would McLuhan say about eBooks? Are eBooks functional? Explain your answers.

6. How would Freud and Marx explain the eBooks phenomenon? What would they say about self-publishing?

14.

Sociability

The Facebook Icon

Facebook Logo

The Facebook icon is a lower case "f" shown in white on a blue background or blue on a white background. There are hundreds of thousands of apps that have been created for smartphones, tablets, and computers, but it is reasonable to suggest that the Facebook icon is the most commonly used one—because so many people belong to Facebook. As I explained earlier in the book in my discussion of semiotics, according to C. S. Peirce, one of the founding fathers of semiotics, there are three kinds of signs: icons, that signify by resemblance; indexes, that signify by connection (such as smoke and fire); and symbols, whose meaning has to be learned. Some apps are iconic in nature, such as the apps with drawings of telephones on them that people recognize as an app for making phone calls. The Facebook app is, semiotically speaking,

What Objects Mean, Second Edition by Arthur Asa Berger, 189–197. © 2014 Taylor & Francis. All rights reserved.

a symbol. You have to learn what the "f" stands for. Many apps are symbols, since you can't tell by looking at them what they do, but we still call them icons.

There are now more than a billion people who belong to Facebook, the dominant social media application of our time. After we have registered for Facebook, we access the application on our smartphones and tablets by clicking on a Facebook icon—a simple letter "f"—and we can post comments and images. If you look at Facebook, you see that it is a visual media and images, generally photographs, play a major role. Facebook reflects the fact that modern cultures are no longer logo-centric, based on words, but image-centric, based on images, and those images are mostly photographs. I would suggest we have moved from an era based on digital cameras to one characterized by digital photography, since smartphones and even tablets can now take photographs. A social scientist, Adam N. Joinson, made a study of how people use Facebook and came up with a number of different ways that Facebook members use the site. The abstract of this study, *"Looking up" or "Keeping up with" People? Motives and Uses of Facebook*, reads as follows:

> This paper investigates the uses of social networking site Facebook, and the gratifications users derive from those uses. In the first study, 137 users generated words or phrases to describe how they used Facebook, and what they enjoyed about their use. These phrases were coded into 46 items which were completed by 241 Facebook users in Study 2. Factor analysis identified seven unique uses and gratifications: social connection, shared identities, content, social investigation, social network surfing and status updating. User demographics, site visit patterns and the use of privacy settings were associated with different uses and gratifications.

The reason that Facebook is popular, then, is because it provides so many services to people who belong to it. If you look at the Facebook newsfeed, you see numerous images, and most of them are photographs—often taken with smartphones and posted on the go. We might ask—what sense do we make of all the photographs we see on Facebook, which is 75 percent photographs?

Photographs no longer always tell the truth, not that they necessarily did in the pre-digital camera, pre-Facebook era. For photographers always mediate between the images they take and "reality," and it is what photographers choose to capture in their photos that we have thought, in the past, was a mirror of reality. It is what photographers choose to select to be in an image that we see, not other images they could have taken or other parts of the same image that they cropped that might have told a different story.

Thus, photographic images are implicitly ideological in nature in that they are based on the world-view of the photographer, and because digital images can be manipulated, no images can be more ideological than digital images. Digital cameras, smartphones, and other devices may enhance our ability to capture images to help us remember what we have seen, but they also can be manipulated, so they have lost any claims to being truthful representations of reality.

Photography has always intrigued writers, perhaps because it offers an alternative way of capturing reality from other image systems, such as painting, and from the written word. Susan Sontag, an American cultural critic, discusses various aspects of photography in her book, *On Photography,* published in 1978, before the digital camera age. She writes about what is distinctive about photography (1978:158):

> Photography has powers that no other image-system has ever enjoyed because, unlike the earlier ones, it is *not* dependent on the image maker. However carefully the photographer intervenes in setting up and guiding the image-making process, the process itself remains an optical-chemical (or electronic) one, the workings of which are automatic, the machinery for which will inevitably be modified to provide still more detailed and, therefore, more useful maps of the real. The mechanical genesis of these images, and the literalness of the powers they confer, amounts to a new relationship between image and reality.

Later in the essay she talks about the capacity of photographs to imprison reality, "of making it stand still." When she wrote this, around 40 years ago, people still saw photography as somewhat magical and didn't think much about the way photographers focused their attention on certain things that interested them and neglected other things that didn't.

The fact is, photographs are always selective interpretations of reality, and what they leave out may be more important than what they capture. When we crop a photograph, we are leaving certain parts of it out and focusing attention on the part we are keeping. The process of taking the photograph may be mechanical or electronic, but the choice of what to photograph (and what to post to Facebook) is always made by the photographer, so it is rather naïve to assert that photographs "capture" reality. And now, of course, with digital cameras and digital photo processing programs and apps, while the process of taking the photo may be automatic, the photograph you see is subject to considerable manipulation.

Sontag does make one important point about photographs: they become part of modern information systems and can be used as instruments of control. In the course of a typical day, it is estimated that the average Londoner is photographed 300 times by video cameras, and people living in cities such as New York and Chicago are probably photographed any number of times by video cameras.

Digital cameras, especially those embedded in smartphones, have revolutionized the way people take photographs, for with digital cameras you can immediately see what the photograph you took looks like and delete it if you don't like it. These cameras and other devices can store an incredible number of images on the cards they use. Facebook has no limit as to how many images you can post. Most digital cameras come with an automatic setting, which means they are in essence, when used with the setting on automatic, point-and-shoot cameras; for many people, it is the camera that does all the thinking now. And it is easy to store the images we take on digital cameras on our computers. We can choose which images we like and send them to companies to develop them, and we can send them to friends and relatives as prints or as e-mailed images. Increasingly we take photographs on our smartphones and send them directly to Facebook or Google+ or other social media programs to which we belong.

The quality of the images digital cameras and smartphones take is so high that I now use them to take photos in foreign countries where I write ethnographic tourism studies. If I take 250 or 300 images on a card, I have plenty of images to choose from when I'm selecting images for my books. What digital devices do is destroy the mystery or suspense that was involved with taking photographs on film—for with a conventional film camera, you never knew what a shot you took would look like until it was finally developed.

With digital cameras and smartphones we can all become photo ethnographers and create our own photographic books. We actually do so, in a piecemeal fashion, with our daily posts on Facebook. Because of the high quality of the photographs one can take on iPhones and other smartphones, the sales of digital cameras, particularly entry-level point-and-shoot models, have been plummeting. The way Facebook looks, we can say, is to a considerable extent the result of smartphones now being able to take very good photographs. And thanks to Facebook, along with other social networks and image organization pages such as Picasa, Flikr, and Tumblr, we can publish and share these images with friends and family instantly. We can also use various internet print-on-demand publishers, like www.blurb.com and www.Lulu.com, to publish physical albums at relatively little expense. So we now are experiencing what might be called the "democratization" of photography publishing. Publishing photographs on various sites on the internet is free, and putting out self-published books of photography is now relatively easy and inexpensive. Facebook, Twitter, and sites like Pinterest are now providing visually arresting catalogues of everyday life in the United States and other countries where they can be accessed—of great value to social scientists and others interested in cultural trends.

The digital cameras found on smartphones are now the pre-eminent means of providing images that serve the function of preserving events and experiences for our individual and collective memory. Tourists can now snap hundreds of photographs when they visit scenic places that provide "photo opportunities" and send them directly to Facebook and other sites. These images allow them to recall their experiences in their travels, and share them with friends via Facebook, even while traveling.

Media scholars Jay David Bolter and Richard Grusin write in their book, *Remediation: Understanding New Media*, about the difference between film photography, the kind of photography that was dominant until the development of digital cameras, and digital photography. They write (2000:105):

> If an image is captured with a digital camera, there is no chemical process as with analog photography. Instead, the image is recorded by photosensitive cells and never exists except as bits. Is such an

image a photograph or a computer graphic? If the image began as a conventional photograph and was scanned into the computer and digitally retouched, is it then a photograph or a computer graphic? In what is called digital photography, the result is an image that is advertised as a photograph and meant to be read as such by the viewer. The digital photographer, who captures images digitally, adds computer graphic elements to conventional photographic images, or combines two or more photographs digitally, still wants us to regard the result as part of the tradition of photography. For the photographers and their audiences, digital photography (like digital compositing and animation in traditional film) is an attempt to prevent computer graphic technology from overwhelming the older medium.

It was possible to slightly modify film photographs by retouching them, and there were other things that could be done to them, but it was a difficult process. The "truthfulness" of photographs in the digital age is no longer something we can take for granted, though the photos of cats and dogs and birthday celebrations and what we might describe as "vernacular life" we find on Facebook are not likely to have been doctored. But we must always remember that every image involves an element of choice by the person taking the image. And there are many apps, such as Instagram, that enable photographers to modify or doctor their images to some extent.

We see, then, that the development of digital photography has changed the way we think about photographs and has deprived them of their previous status as mirrors or an objective picture of reality. As I mentioned above, photographs always are subject to the views and perspectives, and sometimes the ideologies, of those taking the photographs. That is, they are selective images of reality, and are thus similar to oil paintings, which always reflect the perspectives of the artists who make these paintings.

What Facebook and other social media have done is make it possible to "publish" our images and make them available to huge numbers of people. Whereas our photographs once ended up in special books we purchased that were designed to hold them, we now can make our images available to large numbers of people with little effort. Smartphones and some digital cameras now come with means for sending images directly to Facebook or other social media, so photography has been transformed from being a private way to take and keep images and has become an extremely popular social form of messaging. At the same time, this service comes at a cost. Facebook retains intellectual property rights on any images posted to its servers, meaning users effectively transfer ownership of their material to Facebook, Inc. Additionally, while Facebook allows you to manage the privacy settings for images and other content posted, it is possible to circumvent these limitations. While Facebook may allow you to share your photographs instantly with friends and family, the images aren't really yours anymore, and they aren't necessarily restricted to those you've shared them with.

Questions for Discussion and Topics for Further Research

1. Are you on Facebook? If so, why? How do you use Facebook and what benefits do you gain from using it? What are its main functions for people? Contrast its manifest and latent functions?

2. How has Facebook changed American society?

3. If images can be manipulated easily, do they help us remember events or do they offer an idealized, personalized, and distorted picture of the past?

4. Do you think we live in a "post-photographic era"? Do digital photos differ significantly from other kinds of computer graphics? Explain your reasoning.

5. Use a digital camera or smartphone camera to record what you do in a typical day and put the photographs on Facebook. After you examine the photographs, what have you left out of importance? Are the photographs truthful or do they offer an idealized picture of your life?

6. Would Marxists see Facebook as a revolutionary phenomenon or as a repressive one?

7. How would Freudians explain the reasons why people post the images they do on Facebook? Are Facebook posters self-promoting exhibitionists or are they interested in sharing and forming some kind of virtual community?

15.
Shape
Milk Cartons

Milk plays an important role in American culture and the American diet. It is a staple of the American diet and part of the classic American easy lunch combination made for countless generations of American kids: peanut butter and jam sandwiches and milk. People in European countries drink milk, but they seem to prefer consuming milk in their numerous cheeses. Milk in many countries is seen as a beverage for babies and young children, not for adults. And now milk is being replaced in the breakfasts of many Americans by soft drinks, which led milk producers to create their famous "Got Milk" campaign to stimulate milk consumption.

What Objects Mean, Second Edition by Arthur Asa Berger, 199–205. © 2014 Taylor & Francis. All rights reserved.

Nicholson Baker's first novel, *The Mezzanine*, can be described as a comic novel about material culture. The book is full of discussions, often of a tangential nature, of all kinds of common objects, and Baker revels in adding long footnotes and discursive asides on toast, carpets, hot air dryers, earplugs, shampoos, and straws, among other things. On the first page of the book he discusses escalators, then moves on to a long footnote on pages 4 and 5 on straws used to sip sodas.

Baker's discussion of milk cartons appears a bit later in the book (1988:42–43):

> I continue to admire the milk carton, and I believe that the change from milk delivered to the door in bottles to milk bought at the supermarket in cardboard containers with peaked roofs was a significant change for people my age—younger and you would have allied yourself completely with the novelty as your starting point and felt no loss; older and you would have already exhausted your faculties of regret on earlier minor transitions and shrugged at this change. Because I grew up as the tradition evolved, I have an awe, still, of the milk carton, which brought milk into supermarkets where all the rest of the food was, in boxes of wax-treated cardboard that said 'Sealtest,' a nice laboratorial word. I first saw the invention in the refrigerator of my best friend Fred's house (I don't know how old I was, possibly five or six): the radiant idea that you tore apart one of the triangular eves of the carton, pushing its wing flaps back, using the stiffness of its own glued seam against itself, forcing the seal inside out, without ever having to touch it, into a diamond-shape opening which became an ideal pourer, a *better* pourer than a circular bottle opening or a pitcher's mouth because you could create a very fine stream of milk very simply, letting it bend over that leading corner, something I appreciated as I was perfecting my ability to pour my own glass of milk or make my own bowl of cereal—the radiant idea filled me with jealousy and satisfaction. I have a single memory of a rival cardboard method in which a paper stopper was

built into one corner of a flat-topped carton; but the triumphant superiority of the peaked roof idea…swept every alternative aside.

Baker is writing about cartons for quarts or half gallons of milk but most milk in supermarkets is sold by the gallon. And the half gallon milk cartons now mostly have bottle tops in the side (near the top of the carton) that you can unscrew to pour milk. The ritual he described is, generally speaking, only available for those purchasing quarts of milk.

Nothing much happens in the novel in terms of action or the movement of characters. The novel is all about the narrator's speculations about shoe laces and hot air dryers and all kinds of other things that are so much a part of our everyday lives, but about which we seldom think. On the back cover, part of the description says the book "casts a dazzling light on our relations with the objects and people we usually take for granted." The comedy in the book comes from Baker's attention to the minutia of everyday lives—to things like pulling the red threads on Band-Aids to open them or stapling thick piles of paper. His mention of staplers is followed by a long footnote on the development of staplers and the difficulties we often face in using them.

Baker directs his gaze upon and describes, in excruciating detail in some cases, the things that we all do, leading the reader to a shock of recognition. He writes about all the trivial little things that are part of our everyday lives and reveals that we are not alone in finding it difficult to open Band-Aids or get off escalators smoothly or open milk cartons. In Europe and many other countries, it is quite difficult to open milk cartons, and my wife and I now bring along a small pair of scissors to do this.

Discursive writing is a comedic technique based on defeating our expectations that a subject will be dealt with logically and coherently. Instead, the writer moves on to other topics and then moves on yet again from them, which, if done well, we find funny. Discursive writing imitates human consciousness, which flits from one thing to another, but in discursive writing the author plays with his readers and leads them by the nose—in this case the mouth—to all kinds of different places.

I was born in 1933, and when I was growing up in Boston, men delivered milk on horse drawn carts, and milk was sold in glass bottles. The glass bottle was superseded by the milk carton, which in turn gave way to the plastic bottle—for gallon bottles of milk in plastic containers seem to be the dominant container size for milk sold at supermarkets.

When we lived in London, in 1973, we used to order six bottles of milk every other day from the milkman. All our neighbors thought we were crazy. In Argentina, milk companies have moved beyond the plastic bottle, and in supermarkets there, milk is often sold in thin plastic bags that hold a liter of milk. You have to puncture them and pour the milk into a plastic container to use it. In the United States, a new plastic gallon container that is easier and cheaper to ship has been developed, and it will probably become the dominant milk container in future years.

In his book, *Packaging: The Sixth Sense,* motivation researcher Ernest Dichter argues that our choices of products and packages is basically emotional, generated by id elements in our psyches, and that one of the more important functions of packaging is to relieve us of the fear of chaos. Consumers feel, Dichter writes, that products sold in regular shaped containers signify protection and security and enable them to escape from the fear of chaos. He mentions the Swedish company Tetrapak, which has created four-sided milk containers that look vaguely like pyramids, symbols of stability. Dichter writes that Tetrapak (1975:35)

> designed an irregular container for milk and other liquids that can be sealed off without pasteurization. Representing and combining irregularity with an unusual, although geometrical shape, it offers an interesting answer to the fear of chaos.

The milk in these Tetrapak containers is irradiated, which explains why they don't need refrigeration. Packaging has, then, a psychological role and the job of attracting us and, in many cases, reassuring us—a task few of us would have thought could be done by a milk container or any other package.

Packaging also is being used by manufacturers to deceive people who purchase their products. In many foods, the size of the package has remained the same while the amount of food in the package has been diminished by a few ounces or so. Packaging is also often wasteful. Many electronic devices come in relatively large packages that are not necessary. Software is an example of an area where manufacturers often put thin disks into relatively large, book-size packages in order to give their products more importance on shelves of stores that sell software, and to suggest the importance of the software being sold.

In an article, "The Kitchen of Meaning," that appeared in *Le Nouvel Observateur* in 1964, Roland Barthes writes about the hidden significance of common objects. He writes (reprinted in *The Semiotic Challenge*, 1988:198):

> To decipher the world's signs always means to struggle with a certain innocence of objects. We all understand our language so "naturally" that it never occurs to us that it is an extremely complicated system, one anything but "natural" in its signs and rules;

in the same way, it requires an incessant shock of observation in order to deal not with the content of messages but with their making: in short the semiologist, like the linguist, must enter the "kitchen of meaning."

What Baker does in his book, we can see from reading Barthes, is to play around with the innocence of objects. When semioticians enter that kitchen of meaning that Barthes describes, and open their refrigerators, one of the things they will no doubt find will be cartons of milk.

Questions for Discussion and Topics for Further Research

1. Read Baker's *The Mezzanine* and write a paper about the social and cultural significance of other objects and artifacts that he deals with.

2. Find other products whose shape has changed over the years and try to figure out the reason for the changes.

3. Do a research paper on the power of packaging. How has packaging been used by companies selling consumer products?

4. Is drinking Coke, Pepsi, or any other soda pop from cans different from drinking it from bottles? Explain your position.

5. Take a common object and offer an analysis of it in Baker's style.

6. In Argentina, milk is generally sold in plastic bags. What does selling milk in plastic bags suggest about the way Argentinians think about milk?

7. How would Freud and psychoanalytic theorists explain the passion for milk among people of all ages in the United States? When I lived in France, my French friends told me that milk is only for children. How does one use psychoanalytic theory to explain the fact that large numbers of Americans, of every age, drink milk.

8. Find a "got milk" print advertisement and analyze it using the theories discussed in the first part of this book.

16.
Diffusion of Innovation
Bagels

Bagels offer an interesting example of the way new products—in this case, a three inch yeast roll that is boiled then baked, shaped like a donut—spread from their place of origin to other places where, over the course of time, certain innovations in the original nature of bagels were created. Diffusion theory, developed and explained by communications scholar Everett Rogers, suggests that there is a structure to the way innovations spread. He did his original work with corn seeds and then extended his analysis to other phenomena.

The basic elements of his theory are as follows:

1. There is the spread (diffusion) of innovations that is communicated to people.

2. Diffusion can be seen as a special kind of communication that focuses on new processes and ideas.

What Objects Mean, Second Edition by Arthur Asa Berger, 207–214. © 2014 Taylor & Francis. All rights reserved.

3. Because of the newness of the ideas or processes being communicated, there is an element of risk in the processes of diffusion.

4. Innovations are spread by communication in certain channels over a period of time to members of some social group.

In their book, *Communication Models for the Study of Mass Communication*, Denis McQuail and Sven Windahl offer four elements in a process of innovation diffusion (1995:74):

Knowledge. The individual is exposed to an awareness of the existence of the innovation and gains some understanding of how it functions.

Persuasion. The individual forms a favourable or unfavourable attitude towards the innovation.

Decision. The individual engages in activities which lead to a choice to adopt or reject the innovation.

Confirmation. The individual seeks reinforcement for the innovation decision he or she has made, but may reverse the previous decision if exposed to conflicting messages about the innovation.

We can use diffusion theory in a general way to deal with bagels. Rogers developed a model which showed the way innovations spread through society. It takes the form of a roughly bell shaped curve that has the following segments in it:

2 %	Innovators
13.5 %	Early Adopters
34 %	Early Majority
34 %	Late Majority
16 %	Laggards

Let me adapt this theory to the spread of bagels from the place where we have reason to believe that they first were created, in Krakow, Poland. The term "bagel" is an Anglicization of the Yiddish term *beugal* or *beygl*. It may come from the Yiddish word *beigen*, to bend. The bakers in Krakow, in the early 1600s, can be considered to be our innovators. According to Leo Rosten in *The Joys of Yiddish,* the first printed mention of the word "bagel" is found in 1610 in the *Community Regulations of Cracow,* which ordered that bagels be given as a gift to women in *childbirth*.

The bagel can be described as an innovation, a new object. Bagels are round yeast rolls that conventionally don't use eggs, that usually are formed by hand with a hole in their centers, and that use malt rather than sugar. They are boiled for several minutes in water that may have certain spices or other ingredients added, and then are baked. This process gives them a hard crust and a chewy inside and a flavor and mouth feel that large numbers of people find addictive. Bagels have increased in size in the United States and now typically have a three inch diameter and have around 300 calories. Bagels are commonly eaten with cream cheese. Two tablespoons of cream cheese adds ten grams of fat to the bagel.

In Rogers's model, the Jews of Krakow and other Jews in Eastern Europe would be the innovators and early adopters. The large scale immigration of Jews from Poland and other Eastern European countries in the 1880s is probably responsible for the introduction of the bagel into American life, and, quite likely, it was first eaten primarily by Jews in the east coast of America who can be seen as early adopters. Over the years, the bagel became incredibly popular with Americans of all religious, socio-economic, and ethnic persuasions and even overtook the donut, for a while, as the most popular breakfast food. In searching for the popularity of bagels on the internet, I found an article by Marty Meitus, "Bagel's Popularity is Rising Like Yeast," that stated, "We eat around three billion bagels a year, compared with four billion donuts and sweet rolls."

An article by Eddy Goldberg, "You've Come a Long Way, Bagel," offers a picture of the spread of bagels in the United States:

According to most mavens (experts), bagels arrived in the U.S. in the 1880s, along with the wave of Jewish immigrants from Eastern Europe and Germany who settled in New York City. While bagels were swallowed up by most New Yorkers, they remained mostly a local phenomenon until the late 1920s. That's when Harry Lender, a Polish baker, set up his bagel factory in New Haven, Conn., putting bagels in supermarkets and introducing frozen bagels.

Another major stage in the evolution of the American bagel came in 1983, when Nord Brue and Mike Dressell founded Bruegger's in Troy, N.Y. At that point, a century after the bagel's arrival, fewer than one-third of Americans had ever tasted one, according to the company. Bruegger's took the neighborhood take-out bagel store and broadened it to the quick-serve destination with a broader menu we know today.

In the following decades, boiled then baked, bagels began their conquest of America, often taking on new variations as they went. But many newcomers were taken in by their soft, doughy roundness. As the bagel's popularity spread in the 1980s and 1990s (abetted by the rapidly expanding number of franchised bagel stores) emergency rooms nationwide reported a spike in hand wounds as mainstream America learned the finer points of bagel slicing. Since then, familiarity (along with a flowering of bagel-slicing devices) has reduced the injury rate among the rising number of bagel lovers worldwide.

By 2002, the U.S. Census Bureau reported more than 3,200 bagel shops nationwide, with annual sales of $1.3 billion and more than 30,000 employees. In 2005, Bruegger's alone had about 250 locations, with about 100 franchisee-owned, producing about 70 million bagels a year with revenues exceeding $150 million.

This article offers us a perspective on the growth in the popularity of bagels that takes us up almost to the present day. The bagel has spread through the world. I recall seeing a sign for bagels during a recent visit to Japan. Bagels are popular wherever one finds Jews; eating bagels with cream cheese and lox is a hallowed tradition among many Jews. They are often served after Saturday morning services in "Kiddush" lunches that allow the Jews to socialize with one another and build a sense of community among members of the congregations.

Many Jewish people who are not affiliated with synagogues maintain their connection with Judaism by eating bagels with cream cheese and lox and other Jewish foods. They are "cultural Jews," who may not have a connection with Jewish institutions but still regard themselves as Jewish and show this by eating bagels, cream cheese, and lox breakfasts.

An American anthropologist, Stanley Regelson, offers a fascinating analysis of the symbolic significance of bagels, cream cheese, and lox. In his article, "The Bagel: Symbol and Ritual at the Breakfast Table (in W. Arens and Susan P. Montague, *The American Dimension: Cultural Myths and Social Realities*), he discusses "the remarkable growth of the custom among American Jews of eating lox and cream cheese on a bagel on Sunday morning" (1976:124). He discusses various taboos in Jewish culture that ask religious Jews not to eat meat and dairy products (and foods made of milk) at the same time. This injunction comes from the Torah where Jews are told not to boil a kid in its mother's milk.

Regelson lists a number of dichotomies found in Judaism, such as sacred and profane, kosher and *treyf* (non-kosher), heaven and earth, male and female, dairy (*milkhik*) and meat (*flesyshik*) that play a role in the daily lives of observant Jews. He uses these topics to support his contention that (1976:133) "the shape of the bagel symbolically represents a navel mediating between the earthly and the divine." He then discusses a Jewish notion that at the end of time, when the Messiah comes, what Jews consider to be sinful behavior, such as eating meat and dairy products together (as, for example, in a cheeseburger) will be acceptable since the Messiah is "him who permits the forbidden."

This discussion is important because it has implications for Regelson's discussion of bagels, lox, and cream cheese (1976:135):

Lox differs from all other preserved fish preparations in one way: It is as red as blood. The glossy redness of the fish, in combination

with the opaque whiteness of the cheese, results in a striking contrast. Indeed, children frequently refuse to eat lox because of its
visual resemblance to raw meat. The coming together of these two
foods produces a visual pun. Although a permitted combination,
lox and cream cheese give the appearance of violating the strong
taboo on mixing *milkik* and *fleshik.*

This suggestion can be supported from another direction since
in many other cultures the ritual use of white and red refers to male
and female respectively. The reference to semen and menstrual
blood, often perceived as the two elements required for conception
in folk biology, lies just beneath the surface of this symbolic
opposition. Indeed, this idea is made almost explicit in the Talmud.
"The white substance...is supplied by the man, from whom come
the child's brain, bones and sinews; the red substance...is supplied
by the woman, from whom comes its skin, flesh and blood."

Regelson, after a bit more discussion, explains that the real
significance of the combination of bagels, lox, and cream cheese
is that they represent, symbolically, the ritual reenactment of the
elimination of all the prohibitions that govern social behavior, which
are a sign that the Messiah has come. The bagel, lox, and cream
cheese eaters are not aware of the full significance of what they are
doing. He suggests that eating their bagels, lox, and cream cheese,
Jews, of all kinds, are affirming their Jewish identity by (1976:137)
"confirming their adherence to the fundamental structure of a
Messianic faith....In short, it is an unconscious expression of
religiosity and ethnic identity."

Regelson's analysis may seem far-fetched to people who are not
familiar with the curious tricks symbols play and with the complex-
ity of the unconscious and how it applies to Jews and their complex
and tangled relationships with their religion. A non-Jew who eats
a bagel with lox and cream cheese is just having a good, tasty, and
highly calorific meal. From a psychoanalytic perspective, when Jews
eat a bagel with lox and cream cheese, in addition to reflecting an

unconscious need to affirm their religious identity, it may also reflect a desire to escape from the burdens of the Jewish dietary laws by eating something that seems (lox equals meat) to violate these laws. It is what Freud would call an "id experience" that violates the strictures of our superegos, which tell us to avoid highly calorific foods. A four and a half inch bagel has around 340 calories. Three ounces of lox has around 100 calories, and one tablespoon of cream cheese has around 50 calories. So the combination comes to almost 400 calories, assuming you don't pile more than three ounces of lox on your bagel or spread more than 50 calories of cream cheese on it. We satisfy the superego by justifying our behavior as showing our attachment, however distant, to our Judaism. Freud suggested that the child is the father of the man. It is reasonable to argue that the taste of the bagels we ate when we were children became "imprinted" on us (to use Clotaire Rapaille's term) and thus play an important role in our lives when we are adults, allowing us to regress, momentarily, and unconsciously remember the happy days of our childhoods when we experienced unconditional love.

Semiotically speaking, for Jews the bagel, lox, and cream cheese combination may be seen as a signifier of Jewishness in one's background but not necessarily one's attachment to Judaism. Large numbers of Jews do not belong to synagogues and have little to do with Judaism except in terms of eating foods that they ate when they were growing up. The foods we ate when we were children play an important role in our lives when we are older.

Sociologists make a distinction between the manifest or obvious meaning of an action and the latent or hidden meaning of an action. For Jews, the manifest function of eating a bagel with lox and cream cheese may be to satisfy hunger or affirm one's connection with one's Jewish cultural identity, but the latent function often involves sociability, since bagels, cream cheese, and lox are often served at *kiddushes* (brunches) that are held after Saturday morning services in many Jewish synagogues, and thus bagels, cream cheese, and lox may help connect people to one another and reinforce the connections they already have.

Questions for Discussion and Topics for Further Research

1. How do you explain the popularity of the bagel with non-Jews?

2. Find countries now that do not have bagels? How do you explain that?

3. How have bagels evolved? Are the new kinds of bagels a sign of progress or the reverse? Explain your position.

4. Does Regelson's analysis of bagels, cream cheese, and lox seem reasonable to you or far-fetched? Explain your position.

5. What uses and gratifications do people get from eating bagels and lox? What functions does eating bagels and lox have for people, in general, and for Jewish people, in particular?

6. Semiotically speaking, trace the denotations and connotations of bagels, lox, and cream cheese.

7. Contrast and compare, using all the theories discussed in this book, the bagel and the donut, and the people partial to one or the other.

8. Play the myth model game and use the bagel as the example of everyday life behavior.

9. The bagel is only one example of food from a single ethnic community becoming food for the dominant culture. Other examples include burritos, sushi, and tikka masala. Have any foods of your subculture been globalized like this? How do you feel about others using your foodways without knowing the culture behind them?

17.
Narratives
Japanese Manga

Narratives play an important role in our lives. As I define them, narratives are stories, generally with a linear or sequential structure, which pervade our media, our popular culture, our conversations, and our dreams. The commercials we watch on television are generally narratives and so are the comic strips we read in the daily newspaper and the television dramas we tune into and the movies we watch in theatres or at home. Jokes are narratives and so are songs. Our dreams, Freud suggested, are a collection of images that we turn into narratives when we recount them. So we spend a great deal of time watching and listening to narratives.

Laurel Richardson, who has written extensively on narratives, explains their significance to us (1990:118): "Narrative is the primary way through which humans organize their experiences into temporally meaningful episodes.... Narrative is both a mode of reasoning and a mode of representation. People can 'apprehend' the world narratively and people can 'tell' about the world narratively." She adds, "According to Jerome Bruner (1986) narrative reasoning is one of the two basic and universal human cognition modes."

I would like to examine a special kind of narrative—the kind found in Japanese manga comic books. In her article, "Growing Up Japanese Reading Manga," Kinko Ito describes the size of the manga industry in Japan (2004:392):

> Manga is truly a huge and lucrative business in Japan. According to *1999 Shuppan Shishyo Nempo* (1999 Nempo), there were 278 different comic magazines (weekly, monthly, special issues, extra issues, etc.) in 1998, with total circulation of 1.47 billion copies and sales of approximately US$ 5.4 billion. Sales of comic books alone topped US$ 2.3 billion. Manga is an affordable popular entertainment that makes up 34 percent of the Japanese book/magazine market.

In 2012, sales of manga were considerably higher:

> The market research firm Oricon reported that sales of compiled book volumes (*tankōbon*) of manga dipped 1.5% to 267.5 billion yen (about US$2.886 billion) in 2012, compared to the year before. This is the first recorded sales drop since Oricon began taking annual statistics on book sales in Japan in 2009.
>
> (www.animenewsnetwork.com/news/2013-02-03/oricon/ manga-volume-sales-dipped-1.5-percent-in-japan-in-2012)

Ito points out that children as early as three years of age read manga, though generally children are between five and eight when they start reading them, and manga are also popular with many aged Japanese. They are, for the Japanese, an important agent of socialization. As Ito explains, "as the Japanese read manga and experience various events,

social situations, and emotions vicariously, they not only entertain themselves, but also learn social skills and gain pragmatic information and knowledge that are necessary for everyday life" (392–393).

There are countless genres of manga, covering everything from sports, professions, and romance to sex—and some of the sexual portrayals in manga are very detailed. There is also a great deal of violence in many manga, which is interesting because the Japanese people are not violent, as a rule. In recent years, as the Japanese birth rate has declined, so has the sale of manga. In the eighties, when manga were very popular, the statistics are remarkable. In an article about manga in the eighties, "Aspects of the Development Towards a Visual Culture in Respect of Comics: Japan," Lee Loveday and Satomi Chiba (1986:158) offer some statistics about the popularity of manga in 1986. Their article appeared in *Comics and Visual Culture*.

300	Types of regularly produced manga
272 million	Issues of weekly comics sold
930 million	Comic magazines sold in 1981
13%	Amount of weekly allowance spent by high school children on manga
42%	Of Japanese high school children's book collections are manga

It was also estimated that Japanese blue collar workers spend around a third of their leisure time reading manga. We can suggest, then, that although the Japanese people read a great deal, much of what they read are manga.

In 1986, when Loveday and Chiba wrote their article, there were more than 90 erotic manga with titles such as *Sexy Action, Manga Strong,* and *Gekiga Butcher,* manga characterized by "intense, often sordid realism frequently focusing upon lust and violence." They explain the significance of manga in the following manner:

> The fundamental sociopsychological motive that can be attributed to the comic medium's success is its instant provision of escape from frustration and monotony into a sensorily exciting, self-affirming dream world. The charm is achieved by turning the reader into a voyeur of almost film-like action and forcing his immersion into the experiences of the characters through emotionalized and highly dynamic situations of tension. (1986:168)

The Japanese spend long periods of time commuting, and the manga help them escape from the boredom and monotony of travel. As a result of their infatuation, if not obsession, with manga, the Japanese now live in what they describe as an "eyesight culture" that is dominated by visual phenomena—what they call *shikakubunka.* The fact that manga represent around a third of all books sold in Japan suggests that while Japan has a very high literacy rate (and manga may play a role in helping Japanese children learn the language), much of what the Japanese public reads does not have a very high literary quality, though there are some manga that are significant works of art.

There is a tradition of pornographic art work in Japanese culture, so seeing sexually explicit representations of sexual relationships is not new. One fascinating erotic Japanese image shows an octopus having sex with a woman, with its various tentacles caressing her breasts and one penetrating her vagina. It is reasonable to suggest that there are intertextual relationships between ancient Japanese pornographic illustrations and what one finds in manga.

Edward Reischauer and Marius B. Jansen speculate about the cultural significance of manga in their book, *The Japanese Today* (1994:222–223):

> Once Japanese could be seen reading everywhere, on trains, in waiting rooms, and wherever else the situation allowed. They might have been called the "readingest" people in the world. But many of these former readers are now engrossed in the pictures and inarticulate grunts of cartoons. Originally limited to children, their popularity spread to college students, and now sedate businessmen and housewives can be seen devouring them. They run from imaginative adventure stories of all types to equally diverse stories of love or pornographic appeal. What this all means is hard to fathom: a broadening of the public attracted to print, a lessening of the attention span and a lowering of taste produced by television, a revulsion against serious reading by people overburdened by the pressures of school and the workplace, or a sign of the vulgarization of mass society.

It is possible to suggest that all of the reasons the authors give are correct, but now people all over the world read manga because they obtain important gratifications from doing so. Ito found, when she was interviewing Japanese people about their attitudes toward manga, that the Japanese felt very strongly about manga and often bonded with one another over their love of a particular kind of manga. In addition, she explained, "many interesting manga stories have the effect of drugs and soap operas on paper: they are highly addictive" (2004:402). Like video games, manga become addictive because they offer readers increasingly satisfying gratifications that they seek.

It is possible to adopt a "Uses and Gratifications" approach to manga to help us understand why they are so popular. This approach, sociological in nature, focuses not on the effects of exposure to manga (or other kinds of texts in other media) but on the way people who are attracted to these texts use them. Let me suggest some of the more important uses and gratifications that manga supply.

- *To be amused.* Manga entertain their readers with narratives that interest them.

- *To experience extreme emotions in a guilt-free setting.* Many manga are full of violence and sexuality, but readers don't feel any guilt in reading these texts.

- *To find distraction and diversion.* The stories in manga draw people into their own world and let readers escape, if only for a short while, from the burdens and worries of their everyday life.

- *To obtain outlets for sexual drives in a risk-free manner.* The sexuality that plays a major role in many manga speak to and help assuage the sexual drives and desires of the readers.

- *To share experiences with others.* People who read the same manga can talk about them, the same way that people who watch the same television programs often talk about the shows they've seen.

From a Freudian psychoanalytic perspective, manga are "id" texts which escape the strictures of the superego because they are works of fiction, which enables the egos of manga readers to ward off strictures from their superegos by suggesting that manga are works of art that function as a kind of catharsis and enable readers to deal with their sexual drives in a culturally acceptable manner. One might even suggest that manga are similar to dreams and, as such, provide scholars with valuable insights into the Japanese psyche.

Like so many other aspects of Japanese culture manga have spread to other cultures, and in 2007, manga fans in America spent $200 million on manga. The spread of manga and Japanese anime can be understood in terms of theories about the diffusion of innovation. Manga play a significant role in the spread of Japanese popular culture throughout the world, as people everywhere, now, read manga, follow anime, play Japanese video games on Japanese video consoles, and dine in Japanese restaurants. There is what might be called a kind of Japanese popular cultural imperialism as Japanese manga and other Japanese pop cultural products become globally important. While I was in Japan I made a number of short videos of topics like festivals, street food, and manga that I put on YouTube. It is only the videos on manga that seem to be of interest to people. I often receive messages about the manga video from people who write things like "paradise" or "I'm dying to go there." These messages suggest that manga play a role in the lifestyle of people in the United States and, no doubt, in other countries as well.

Questions for Discussion and Topics for Further Research

1. What roles do narratives play in your life? How many narratives are you exposed to in a typical day? What kinds of narratives are dominant?

2. Investigate the popularity of manga in Japan now. The sale of manga is decreasing in Japan in recent years. Why might that be?

3. With whom are manga popular in the United States? What is the reason for their appeal to people in America? Are Americans reading manga or are they primarily popular with Japanese people living in the United States?

4. How might psychoanalytic theorists explain the popularity of ultra-violent and/or hyper-sexualized manga in an otherwise non-violent, conservative culture such as Japan's? Do some research on this matter on articles and books by psychoanalytic theorists.

18.

Nationalism

The American Flag

Nationalism can be defined, roughly speaking, as the powerful emotional attachment people have towards the country, and its history, institutions, and core values, in which they are born and grow up. In his book, *The Culture Code*, Clotaire Rapaille explains that children between the ages of one and seven are "imprinted" with their culture and these imprints shape their behavior to a considerable degree. He writes (2006:22):

> Most of us imprint the meanings of the things most central to our lives by the age of seven. This is because emotion is the central force for children under the age of seven...most people are exposed to only one culture before the age of seven. They spend most of their time at home or within their local environment....The extremely

What Objects Mean, Second Edition by Arthur Asa Berger,
223–231. © 2014 Taylor & Francis. All rights reserved.

strong imprints placed in their subconscious at this early age are determined by the culture in which they are raised. An American child's most active period of learning happened in an American context. Mental structures formed in an American environment fill his subconscious. The child therefore grows up an American. This is why people from different cultures have such different reactions to the same things. Let's take, for example, peanut butter. Americans receive a strong emotional imprint from peanut butter. Your mother makes you a peanut-butter-and-jelly sandwich when you are young, and you associate it with her love and nurturance.

Rapaille offers us an insight into how the powerful emotions connected with one's country become formed. He offers an example of peanut butter. Rapaille was raised in France, and thus peanut butter didn't play a role in his life, but cheese played a major role in his life, since the French are passionate about cheese. Also champagne. My point is that as we grow up we develop very strong emotional attachments to the country in which we are born or in which we spend our early, formative years.

In Ralph Ross and Ernest van den Haag's *The Fabric of Society: An Introduction to the Social Sciences,* there is an excellent explanation of nationalism (1957:626):

The word "nation" comes from *natus*...to be born. A nation was a group of cognates, of kindred people born on the same soil and into the same group. But the meaning of the word has been extended with the feeling of nationhood. People feel united by bonds of nationhood when they have some of the following: shared historical experience; identical groups felt as outsiders or enemies; common language (this is perhaps most important: it is when people "speak the same language" and "understand one another" that they feel most clearly identified as group members); shared cultural patterns and social institutions; common residence in a particular territory (country); predominance of one ethnic strand.

This passage was written before immigration became widespread and countries became multi-cultural, with people in one country speaking many different languages. In San Francisco, as a result of immigration from many countries, there are now more than 60 native languages spoken by many students in the school system. It is the American school system which "Americanizes" these immigrant children, and this process has been going on since America, a country of immigrants, started opening its borders to people from other countries.

We gain another perspective on nationalism in a more recent work, *Cultural Theory: The Key Concepts,* by Andrew Edgar and Peter Sedwick. They point out that nationalism has a strong cultural component to it (2008:220):

> Nationalism presents itself not simply as a political phenomenon, but also as a matter of cultural identity. As such, any conception of the national to which it refers must take account of the ethnic, historic and linguistic criteria, as well as political notions such as legitimacy, bureaucracy and presence of definable borders.... Nationalism thus defined is a modern phenomenon, becoming prevalent towards the end of the eighteenth century...the development of nationalism is concomitant with the development of the modern state, primarily in Europe and North America. The dates of the American Declaration of Independence (1776) and the French Revolution (1789) are frequently cited as marking the beginning of nationalism.

Mulford Q. Sibley, a political scientist, explains how nationalism took on a religious quality. He writes, in *Political Ideas and Ideologies: A History of Political Thought* (1970:556–557):

> As traditional religions declined, nationalism often took their place, becoming the effective final commitment for millions of human beings. Carlton Hayes rightly points out that a "religion of nationalism" came to characterize almost every modern state. Sometimes aided and abetted by high toned philosophers and in

most areas encouraged by journalism, official propaganda, and popular culture, this religion had its own martyrs, priests, rituals and appeals to the irrational. Its martyrs were those who had died in wars of national liberation, its priests the intellectuals and journalists who developed its mystiques. Its rituals consisted of patriotic exercises, rigidly defined ceremonies for paying homage to the flag, gun salutes for presidents and kings, national holy days, religious services at tombs of unknown soldiers, and national creeds repeated by rote.

Sibley calls our attention to the powerful emotional attachment people make to their countries and to the way their countries instill this attachment in their citizens. We can think of nationalism as having religious-like significance to people.

We can see this is the "Pledge of Allegiance" that American children recite in schools. It reads

"I pledge allegiance to the Flag of the United States of American and to the republic for which it stands, one Nation, under God, indivisible, with liberty and justice for all."

The pledge was written by Francis Bellamy in 1892 and has been modified four times, the latest being in 1954 when the phrase "under God" was inserted in the pledge. Children in American schools generally recite the pledge at the beginning of the school day, with their right hand over their hearts. The pledge is to the American flag, which is a signifier of the American republic. Semiotically speaking, a flag is a symbolic 'metonym,' a means of communication in which a part stands for the whole. For example, the White House is a metonym for the American presidency and the Pentagon for the American armed forces. The American flag, then, is a metonym for American society and culture and American life, in general. This pledge to the American flag leads to the next topic I will discuss, the symbolic significance of the American flag.

The first American flag was authorized by the Continental Congress when it passed the Flag Act on June 14, 1777. There have been a number of different versions of the flag until the present one with 13 horizontal stripes (seven red and six white) and 50 stars in a blue canton was authorized. Some other ideas for the American flag are shown below:

We can see there have been many notions about what the American flag should look like over the years. One thing we notice about all of these variations is that they have red and white stripes and a blue area with stars or some other image.

The red color in the American flag stands for valor, the white stands for purity, and the blue stands for justice. Every June 14th, on the anniversary of the first flag act on June 14, 1777, Americans celebrate Flag Day and display their flags. When our astronauts landed on the moon, they planted an American flag, as a sign that America had been to the moon first—not because we had a sense of wanting to colonize it, which is one of the traditional uses of flags. Although Americans

honor the flag, we are not averse to using it on t-shirts and other gar-
ments, and we even have postage stamps with the American flag on
them. Many countries do not allow their flags to be used in these ways
because they feel that doing so devalues the flag and is an insult to the
country whose flag is so used. For these countries, the flag is something sacred. The American flag is also sacred for Americans, but we
are allowed to use images of the flag in any way we wish. This may be
because we make a distinction between the flag itself and images of
the flag. Images of the flag can be seen as a kind of speech or artistic
expression and thus protected by the Constitution.

A book, *Blood Sacrifice and the Nation: Totem Rituals and the
American Flag*, makes a radical argument about the role of the flag in
American culture. The authors, C. Marvin and D. W. Ingle, suggest
that patriotism in American is a political religion involving blood sacrifice and that America continually kills its children (young men and
women soldiers) to keep the country unified. The flag is the sacred
symbol of this religion and the sacrifices made in its name. Here are
several passages from the book (1999):

> The underlying cost of all society is the violent death of some of
> its members. OUR DEEPEST SECRET, THE COLLECTIVE GROUP
> TABOO, IS KNOWLEDGE THAT SOCIETY DEPENDS ON THE
> DEATH OF THESE SACRIFICIAL VICTIMS *AT THE HANDS OF THE
> GROUP ITSELF.*

> We argue that the flag is the god of nationalism, and its mission is
> to organize death.

> Durkheim says, "If a belief is unanimously shared by a people, then
> it is forbidden to touch it, that is to say, to deny or to contest it. Now
> the prohibition of criticism is an interdiction like the others and
> proves the presence of something sacred."

> The flag is the only proper casket covering in funerals with military
> honors. In war, the group ritually kills the very tribe members who

otherwise enjoy protected status. In this protected status, group members are taboo like the flag, and for the same reason. They embody the group in their persons. The flag signifies the special condition of sacrifice, of lifting the killing taboo for the sake of the group. Only the flag signifies the sacrificed body. The flag is treated both as a live being and as the sacred embodiment of a dead one. The sacrificed body is resurrected in the flag.

We are concerned with enduring groups whose members will shed blood in their defense. To join an enduring group is to commit to a system of organized violence. This lesson is difficult and repugnant. Our refusal to recognize the contribution of violence to the creation and maintenance of enduring groups is the totem taboo at work.

This analysis is based upon a combination of anthropological theory about the nature of ritual killings and taboos and psychoanalytic theory, which suggests we often refuse to recognize the real significance of things we do. The American flag becomes, we see, an incredibly powerful symbol that is connected to our willingness to sacrifice young men and women for the sake of the solidarity of the nation. This willingness is at the unconscious level, of course. We are not aware of the hidden meanings of the flag.

The powerful feelings we have about the flag, which starts with the association between the flag and American society found in the Pledge of Allegiance, may explain the outrage many people feel when some Americans, protesting various aspects of American life and politics, burn an American flag. The Supreme Court has ruled that burning the American flag is an example of free speech that is protected by the United States Constitution and so Americans are free to burn the flag if they desire to do so, though most Americans find this behavior distasteful and repugnant, to put it mildly. In many countries in the Middle East, groups that dislike our foreign policy often burn American flags, as a means of showing their hatred of all things American. Many Americans feel the same kind of repugnance towards these flag burnings, invariably captured on video and shown on news programs, as they do about Americans burning American flags.

Many Americans also feel quite negative about another flag that is popular in some southern states, the flag used during the Civil War by the Confederate soldiers. It has a blue diagonal cross with 13 stars on the cross and has a red background. It was designed by William Porcher Miles, who hoped it would be adopted as the American flag, but the flag we have now, the "Stars and Strips," was chosen instead. The Confederate flag is connected to memory—of the Civil War and the many southerners who died in that terrible war. It is a symbol, then, of the regionalism that exists in countries and always poses problems. For black Americans, the Confederate flag is a symbol of slavery that was found in the South (and to some degree in the North) before the Emancipation Proclamation freed all slaves in the United States. Many Americans see the Confederate flag as a provocation and a symbol of the reluctance of many people in the American south have to accept the fact that the South lost the Civil War and that the social arrangements at the time are no longer acceptable. So flags can unify people in a nation, but they can also divide them. Even now, 150 years after the Civil War, there are people in some states who harbor dreams—most would say delusions—about seceding from the United States and forming a new country.

Questions for Discussion and Topics for Further Research

1. Investigate the history of the American flag and the various changes in its design over the years.

2. How do flags affect people emotionally? What is the secret of their power?

3. Do some research on separatist movements in the United States and attempts people have made, over the years, to set up separate countries. Look into whether they created their own flags.

4. What do political scientists and psychologists say about patriotism and exposure to the American flag? Does the flag generate nationalism or patriotism or both?

5. How would Freudians and psychoanalytic theorists explain the attachment people have for their country's flags and the people who burn flags?

Part III
Material Culture Games

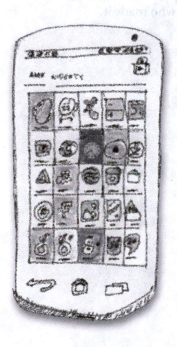

The Artifacts Inventory Game

Please list 24 artifacts and objects you own (electronic gizmos, fashion items, cosmetics, and so forth) in the chart, being specific about their brands. After you have made this list, what do you think it reflects about you as a person? Please write your initials on the list and pass your list in to your professor, who will shuffle the lists and distribute them to your classmates. The object of the game is to see what one of your classmates finds interesting about the list and what it reflects about the person who made it.

What Objects Mean, Second Edition by Arthur Asa Berger, 234–252. © 2014 Taylor & Francis. All rights reserved.

1.	2.	3.
4.	5.	6.
7.	8.	9.
10.	11.	12.
13.	14.	15.
16.	17.	18.
19.	20.	21.
22.	23.	24.

The Time Capsule Game

According to *The Random House Dictionary of the English Language: The Unabridged Edition,* a time capsule is "a receptacle containing documents or objects typical of the current period placed in the earth in a cornerstone, etc. for discovery in the future." We will limit ourselves to relatively simple objects. You must decide which objects best reflect American culture of recent years.

Make a list of the 15 objects you would put in a time capsule if you were going to bury one on campus today. In selecting the objects for the time capsule, you should be mindful of the following considerations:

1. Are the objects representative of American society?

2. Are you avoiding unconscious bias of one kind or another?

3. Will people digging up the time capsule in 50 or 100 years be able to make sense of the objects you've placed in it?

4. Are you covering the most important categories of objects?

5. You should include foods, beverages, media devices, and so forth.

6. Put objects in the capsule in order of their importance.

1.	2.	3.
4.	5.	6.
7.	8.	9.
10.	11.	12.
13.	14.	15.

Disciplinary Perspectives on Objects Exercise

In this exercise, we apply concepts that semioticians, sociologists, psychoanalytic theorists, and Marxists would use to analyze various objects. A list of some important concepts and theories follows. Your task is to decide which concepts are the best to use to analyze the object. Explain your use of each of the concepts that you apply to a given object.

Unconscious	Sign	Alienation
Id	Signifier	Class Conflict
Ego	Signified	Ruling Class
Superego	Icon	False Consciousness
Conscious	Index	Conspicuous Consumption
Preconscious	Functional	Protestant Asceticism
Oedipus Complex	Disfunctional	Iron Cage
Defense Mechanisms	Latent Functions	Aura
Ambivalence	Manifest Functions	Authenticity
Denial	Race	Postmodernism
Fixation	Ethnicity	Modernism
Identification	Gender	Culture Codes
Rationalization	Hierarchical Elitists	Grid-Group Theory
Regression	Individualists	Myth
Suppression	Egalitarians	Sacred
Oral	Fatalists	Profane
Anal	Needs	Functional Alternative
Phallic	Desires	Culture
Genital	Fashion	Taste Culture

Disciplinary Perspectives on Objects

Object	Psychoanalytic	Semiotic
Big Mac		
iPod		

Object	Sociological	Marxist
Birkenstocks		
Bic shaver		

The Grid-Group Theory and Objects Game

Grid-Group Theory, as explained earlier in the book, argues that there are four lifestyles that shape our purchases. Find objects to place in appropriate slots for each lifestyle. Justify all your choices and be specific about brands.

Object	Hierarchical Elitist	Competitive Individualists	Egalitarian	Fatalist
Books	*The Prince*	*Looking Out for Number One*	*I'm Okay, You're Okay*	*Down and Out in Paris and London*
Blue Jeans				
Running Shoes				
Magazines				
Music CDs				
Cell Phones				
Watches				
Your choice				

The Objects and Personal Identity Game

In this game, your instructor will give everyone in the class identical small brown paper bags. You are to put in the bag an object that you think reflects your personality. On a piece of paper, write your name and list the attributes that you think the artifact reflects about you.

The game is played as follows. Your instructor will show the object to the class, and everyone will try to discern what attributes are reflected in the object. What will be interesting to see is whether what the class finds in the objects is similar to what you have written about yourself in the list you made.

Let me offer an example. When I played a similar game with my class (they could use anything they wanted), one woman placed an empty sea shell about six inches long in her bag. When I asked the class what it reflected, they came up with terms such as "empty," "sterile," and "dead." The terms she had written on her list were "natural," "simple," and "beautiful." The moral of this exercise is that the messages we think we're sending to people by the way we dress and the objects we use aren't necessarily being interpreted correctly by those who receive these messages.

The Signifying Objects Game

In this game, I list some concepts (technically speaking, signifieds), such as love, hate, and alienation, and ask you to find objects (technically speaking, signifiers) that reflect the concept. In some cases, you will need a combination of objects/signifiers to play the game. This game can be assigned as homework, but it works very well in class, with teams of three students playing the game. You must have a clear definition of each concept in your mind when you play this game. I offer as an example: Secret Agent.

Signifying Objects

Secret Agent	Romantic Love	Hate	Anxiety
Gun with silencer			
Slouch hat			
Fast sports car			
Alienation	**French-ness**	**Horror**	**Terror**
American-ness	**Narcissism**	**Power**	**Your Choice**

Disciplinary Writing Exercise

Pretend you are a writer for one (at a time) of these journals and make an analysis using concepts and theories appropriate to that journal for an object that you own. I suggest you do a semiotic analysis for *Signs in Society* and choose one other one. Make sure you use a number of the important concepts in each discipline you choose. Which of the two analyses was most difficult to write? Which was most revealing?

Semiotic	*Signs in Society*
Marxist	*Class Confrontations*
Freudian	*Psyche and Society*
Sociological	*Social Knowledge*
Anthropological	*Culture Codes*
Archaeological	*Artifactia*

When you are asked to write two different interpretations of the same object for these magazines you can see that analyses don't just come out of the blue but are grounded in a writer's approach to things. If you found this exercise interesting, you can choose two others and write four different disciplinary analyses of the same object.

The Analyzing Artifact Advertisements Game

Below I offer a list of topics to consider when analyzing print advertisements. Use this list to analyze the advertisements that follow. Consider, also, how people with different disciplinary perspectives might view the advertisement.

Your instructor might ask you to find other advertisements to analyze on your own. I usually break my class into teams of three persons and ask them to see what they can find in a given advertisement. I give them five or ten minutes to make their analysis. Then I pass the advertisement on to another team and see what they find. After two or three teams have completed their analysis, we then discuss what each team has found in the advertisement. This list is adapted from my book *Ads, Fads and Consumer Culture*. You won't have to apply all of these considerations to a given advertisement, but the list provides a number of things to think about when analyzing advertisements.

Graphic Design
1. How would you describe the graphic design of the advertisement?

Amount of Copy
2. How much copy is there relative to the amount of pictorial matter? Is this relationship significant in any respect?

Use of White Space
3. Is there a great deal of blank (white) space in the advertisement, or is it full of graphic and textual material? What does that mean?

Use of Color in Ad
4. If the photograph is in color, what colors dominate? What significance do you think these colors have?

People Shown in Ad

5. How would you describe the figures in the advertisement? Consider facial expression, hair color, hair length, hair styling, fashions, and so on.

Narrative Aspects Implied in Ad

6. What is happening in the advertisement? What does the "action" in the photo suggest?

Semiotic Aspects: Signs, Signifiers, Icons, Indexes, Symbols

7. Are there any signs or symbols in the photograph? If so, what role do they play?

Use of Language and Rhetorical Devices

8. How is language used? What arguments are made and rhetorical devices used?

Significance of Typefaces

9. What impressions do you get from each of the different typefaces used in the advertisement?

Theme of Ad

10. What are the basic "themes" in the advertisement? How do these themes relate to the story implied by the advertisement?

Target Audience of Ad

11. What product or service is being advertised? Who is the target audience for this product or service?

Cultural Values and Beliefs Reflected in Ad

12. What values and beliefs are reflected in the advertisement? Sexual jealousy? Patriotism? Motherly love? Brotherhood of man? Success? Power? Good taste?

Background Information Needed to Understand Ad

13. Is there any background information you need to make sense of the advertisement?

Advertisements to Analyze

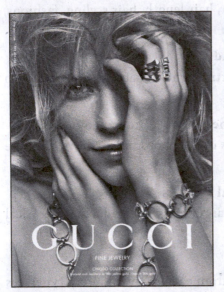

The Id/Ego/Superego Game

In this game, I offer a number of different kinds of objects for you work with. Using Freud's theories about the id, ego, and superego, place specific objects, with brand names, in each slot in the chart. Remember that Freud suggested that the id reflects desire and lust, the ego represents knowing reality and mediates between the id and superego, and the superego represents guilt and conscience. The objects may not all fit perfectly, so we can say they represent id-like, ego-like, and superego-like aspects of our psyches. Be specific about the titles of books, video games, and so forth.

Id/Ego/Superego Objects

Topic	Id	Ego	Superego
Books			
Video Games			
Magazines			
Fragrances			
Music Albums			
Soft Drinks			
Your Choice			

The Functions of Objects Game

In my discussion of functionalism, I pointed out that sociologists use the term to mean something that contributes to the maintenance of whatever institution it is found in. If something causes problems to the entity in which it is found, we say it is disfunctional. And if it plays no role, we say it is non-functional. In addition, sociologists use the term "manifest function" to describe the purpose for which the entity was created and "latent function" to describe the unintended and unrecognized function of the entity. Sociologists also use the term "functional alternatives" to describe other ways of doing something. In this game, I provide an object and ask you to deal with its manifest and latent functions and with functional alternatives to it.

Functions of Objects

Object	Manifest function	Latent function	Functional alternative
Coca-Cola			
iPod			
Bud Light			
Chanel No. 5			
Bikini			
Blue Jeans			
Your Choice			

The Myth Model Game

In this game we take a myth and find an object that is connected to it, similar to what I did earlier with the myth of Prometheus and cigarette lighters. Here are some important Biblical stories and myths to consider:

David and Goliath	Jonah and the Whale
Narcissus	Samson
Hercules	Achilles
Adam and Eve	Midas
Cupid	Orpheus
Tower of Babel	Theseus and Minotaur
Icarus	Noah's Ark
Medusa	Mercury
Odysseus	Oedipus
Sisyphus	Dionysus

If you can't find items to completely fill out the model, don't let that stop you from playing the game. The important thing is to find a connection between a myth or Biblical story and an everyday life object.

	Myth 1	Myth 2	Myth 3	Myth 4
Myth				
Psycho-analytic Theory				
Historical Events				
Elite Culture				
Popular Culture				
Everyday Life				

References

Ante, Spencer E.
"Smartphone Upgrades Slow as 'Wow' Factor Fades,"
  July 17, 2013, B1.
Wall Street Journal.

Baker, Nicholson. 1988.
The Mezzanine.
New York: Weidenfeld & Nicholson.

Bakhtin, M. M. (trans. C. Emerson and M. Holquist). 1981.
The Dialogic Imagination.
Austin: University of Texas Press.

Barthes, Roland (trans. Annette Lavers). 1972.
Mythologies.
New York: Hill and Wang.

Barthes, Roland (trans. Richard Howard). 1982.
Empire of Signs.
New York: Hill and Wang.

Barthes, Roland (trans. Richard Howard). 1988.
The Semiotic Challenge.
New York: Hill and Wang.

Bateson, Gregory. 1972.
Steps to an Ecology of Mind.
New York: Ballantyne.

Baudrillard, Jean (trans. James Benedict). 1968/1996.
The System of Objects.
London: Verso.

Benjamin, Walter.
"The Work of Art in the Age of Mechanical Reproduc-tion"
  in Mast, Gerald and Marshall Cohen (eds.)
Film Theory and Criticism. 1974.
New York: Oxford University Press.

Berger, Arthur Asa (ed.) 1974.
About Man: An Introduction to Anthropology.
Dayton, OH: Pflaum/Standard.

Berger, Arthur Asa. 1999.
Signs in Contemporary Culture: An Introduction to Semiotics.
Salem, WI: Sheffield.

Berger, Arthur Asa. 2005.
Shop 'Til You Drop: Consumer Behavior and American Culture.
Lanham, MD: Rowman & Littlefield.

Berger, John. 1978
Ways of Seeing.
London: British Broadcasting System and Penguin Books.

Berger, Peter and Brigitte Berger. 1972.
Sociology: A Biographical Approach.
New York: Basic Books.

Bettelheim, Bruno. 1977.
The Uses of Enchantment.
New York: Vintage.

Bolter, Jay, David and Richard Grusin. 2000.
Remediation: Understanding New Media.
Cambridge, MA: MIT Press.

Boorstin, Daniel. 1961/1975.
The Image: A Guide to Pseudo-Events in America.
New York: Atheneum.

Bosman, Julie.
"E-Book Sales a Boon to Publishers," May 15, 2013.
New York Times.

Bottomore, T. B. and M. Rubel (eds.) (trans. T. B. Bottomore). 1964.
Karl Marx: Selected Writings.
New York: McGraw-Hill.

Brenner, Charles. 1974.
An Elementary Textbook of Psychoanalysis.
Garden City, NY: Doubleday.

Brooks, David.
"Lord of the Memes," August 8, 2008.
New York Times.

Caple, Chris. 2006.
Objects: Reluctant Witnesses to the Past.
New York: Routledge.

Coser, Lewis. 1971.
Masters of Sociological Thought.
New York: Harcourt Brace Jovanovich.

Culler, Jonathan. 1976.
Structuralist Poetics: Structuralism, Linguistics, and the Study of Literature.
New York: Cornell University Press.

Danesi, Marcel. 2002.
Understanding Media Semiotics.
London: Arnold.

Danesi, Marcel (ed.) 2013.
Encyclopedia of Media and Communication.
Toronto: University of Toronto Press.

Dichter, Ernest. 1960.
The Strategy of Desire.
London: Boardman.

Dichter, Ernest. 1975.
Packaging: The Sixth Sense?
Boston: Cahners Books.

Douglas, Mary.
"In Defence of Shopping" in Falk, Pasi and Colin Campbell (eds.)
The Shopping Experience. 1997.
London: Sage.

Doyle, A. Conan. 1975.
The Adventures of Sherlock Holmes.
New York: A & W Visual Library.

Dunham, Deborah.
"The Price of Pretty: Women Spend $50,000 on Hair Over Lifetime."
main.stylelist.com/2010/03/29/the-price-of-pretty-women-spend-50-000-
   on-hair-over-lifetime/

Durham, Meenashiki Gigi and Douglas Kellner (eds.). 2001.
Adventures in Media and Culture Studies: Introducing the KeyWorks.
Malden, MA: Blackwell.

Durkheim, Emile (trans. J. W. Swain). 1915/1965.
The Elementary Forms of Religious Life.
New York: Free Press.

Eco, Umberto. 1976.
A Theory of Semiotics.
Bloomington: Indiana University Press.

Edgar, Andrew and Peter Sedwick (eds.). 2008.
Cultural Theory: The Key Concepts.
New York: Routledge.

Eliade, Mircea (trans. W. R. Trask). 1961.
The Sacred and the Profane: The Nature of Religion.
New York: Harper & Row.

Erikson, Erik. 1963.
Childhood and Society. 2nd Edition.
New York: W. W. Norton.

Ewen, Stuart. 1976.
Captains of Consciousness: Advertising and the Social Roots of Consumer Culture.
New York: McGraw-Hill.

Ewen, Stuart and Elizabeth Ewen. 1982.
Channels of Desire: Mass Images and the Shaping of American Consciousness.
New York: McGraw-Hill.

Fairchild, Henry Pratt. 1966.
Dictionary of Sociology and Related Sciences.
Totowa, NJ: Littlefield, Adams.

Falk, Pasi and Colin Campbell (eds.). 1997.
The Shopping Experience.
London: Sage.

Fishwick, Marshall and Ray B. Browne (eds.). 1970.
Icons of Popular Culture.
Bowling Green, OH: Bowling Green University Popular Press.

Fowler, Geoffrey and Betsy McKay.
"Coke Pins Hopes on Blitz in Beijing," August 19, 2008.
Wall Street Journal.

Freud, Sigmund.
"Psychoanalysis" in Rieff, Philip (ed.)
Freud: Character and Culture. 1963.
New York: Collier.

Freud, Sigmund. 1953.
A General Introduction to Psychoanalysis.
Garden City, NY: Permabooks.

Frisby, David and Mike Featherstone (eds.). 1997.
Simmel on Culture.
London: Sage.

Fromm, Erich. 1962.
Beyond the Chains of Illusion.
New York: Touchstone.

Gamble, Clive. 2005.
Archaeology: The Key Concepts.
London: Routledge.

Gans, Herbert J. 1974.
Popular Culture and High Culture: An Analysis and Evaluation of Taste.
New York: Basic Books.

Geertz, Clifford. 2000.
The Interpretation of Cultures.
New York: Basic Books.

Girard, René. 1991.
A Theater of Envy: William Shakespeare.
New York: Oxford University Press.

Goldberg, Eddy.
"You've Come a Long Way, Bagel."
www.franchising.com/articles/youve_come_a_long_way_bagel.html

Goldman, Robert and Stephen Papson. 1996.
Signs Wars: The Cluttered Landscape of Advertising.
New York: Guilford.

Gottdiener, Mark. 1995
Postmodern Semiotics: Material Culture and the Forms of Postmodern Life.
Cambridge, MA: Blackwell.

Grotjahn, Martin. 1971.
The Voice of the Symbol.
New York: Delta Books.

Hall, Stuart (ed.). 1997.
Representation: Culture Representation and Signifying Practices.
London: Sage.

Haug, Wolfgang. 1987.
Commodity Aesthetics, Ideology & Culture.
New York: International General.

Henry, Jules. 1963.
Culture Against Man.
New York: Vintage Books.

Hinsie, L. E. and R. J. Campbell. 1970.
Psychiatric Dictionary.
New York: Oxford University Press.

Huizinga, Johan. 1924.
The Waning of the Middle Ages.
Garden City, NY: Anchor.

Ito, Kinko.
"Growing Up Japanese Reading Manga," Vol. 6, No. 2, Fall, 2004.
International Journal of Comic Art.

Jensen, Gordon and Luh Ketut Suryani. 1992.
The Balinese People: A Reinvestigation of Character.
New York: Oxford University Press.

Johnson, Wendell. 1946.
People in Quandries.
New York: Harper & Brothers.

Joinson, Adam N.
"Looking up" or "Keeping Up With" People? Motives and Uses of Facebook.
onemvweb.com/sources/sources/looking_at_motives_facebook.pdf

Kang, Stephanie.
"Bottom Lines," September 6, 2006.
Wall Street Journal.

Klapp, Orrin. 1962.
The Collective Search for Identity.
New York: Holt, Rinehart and Winston.

Koenig, Rene. 1973.
The Restless Image: A Sociology of Fashion.
London: George Allen & Unwin.

Lefebvre, Henri. 1971.
Everyday Life in the Modern World.
New Brunswick, NJ: Transaction.

Leroy-Gourhan, Andre. 1964–1966.
Le Geste et la Parole. Two Volumes.
Paris: Albin Michel.

Leung, Louis and Ran Wei.
"More Than Just Talk on the Move: Uses and Gratifications of the Cellular Phone,"
    Summer, 2000.
Journalism and Mass Communications Quarterly.

Loveday, Lee and Satori Chiba.
"Aspects of the Development Towards a Visual Culture" in
Alphons Silbermann (ed.)
Comics and Visual Culture. 1986.
Berlin, Germany: Walter de Gruyter.

Lunenfeld, Peter. 2000.
The Digital Dialectic: New Essays on New Media.
Cambridge, MA: MIT Press.

Lyotard, Jean Francois (trans. G. Bennington and B. Massumi). 1984.
The Postmodern Condition: A Report on Knowledge.
Minneapolis: University of Minnesota Press.

McLuhan, Marshall. 1951.
The Mechanical Bride: Folklore of Industrial Man.
Boston: Beacon.

McLuhan, Marshall. 1965.
Understanding Media: The Extensions of Man.
New York: McGraw-Hill.

McLuhan, Marshall. 1969.
Counterblast.
New York: Harcourt, Brace & World.

McQuail, Denis and Sven Windahl, 1995.
Communication Models for the Study of Mass Communication. 2nd Edition.
New York: Longman.

Malinowski, Bronislaw. 1922/1961.
Argonauts of the Western Pacific.
New York: E. P. Dutton.

Marvin, C. and D. W. Ingle. 1999.
Blood Sacrifice and the Nation: Totems, Rituals and the American Flag.
Cambridge, UK: Cambridge University Press.

Marx, Karl.
"Preface to the Contribution to the Critique of Political Economy" in Bottomore, T.
    B. and M. Rubel (eds.)
Selected Writings in Sociology and Social Philosophy. 1964.
New York: McGraw-Hill.

Mast, Gerald and Marshall Cohen (eds.). 1974.
Film Theory and Criticism: Introductory Readings.
New York: Oxford University Press.

Meitus, Marty.
"Bagels Popularity is Rising Like Yeast."
www.deseretnews.com/article/495005/BAGELS-POPULARITY-IS-RISING-
    LIKE-YEAST.html?pg=all

Moranis, Rick.
"My Days are Numbered," November 22, 2000.
New York Times.

Myers, Greg. 1999.
Ad Worlds.
London: Arnold.

Nietzsche, Friedrich (trans. R. Hollingdale and W. Kauffman). 1968.
The Will to Power.
New York: Random House.

Nuessel, Frank.
"Culture and Communication" in Marcel Danesi
Encyclopedia of Media and Communication. 2013.
Toronto: University of Toronto Press.

Patai. Raphael. 1972.
Myth and Modern Man.
Englewood Cliffs, NJ: Prentice-Hall.

Penn, William. 1693.
Some Fruits of Solitude.
www.quotationpark.com/topics/ornament.html

Rapaille, Clotilde. 2006.
The Culture Code.
New York: Broadway.

Regelson, Stanley.
"The Bagel: Symbol and Ritual" in W. Arens and Susan Montgomery (eds.)
*The American Dream: Cultural Myths and Social Realities.*1976.
Port Washington, NY: Alfred.

Reischauer, Edward and Marius B. Jensen. 1994.
The Japanese Today.
Cambridge, MA: Harvard University Press.

Renfrew, Colin and Paul Patin (eds.). 2005.
Archaeology: The Key Concepts.
London: Routledge.

Rheingold, Howard. 2003.
Smart Mobs: The Next Social Revolution.
Cambridge, MA: Perseus.

Rieff, Philip (ed.). 1963.
Freud: Character and Culture.
New York: Collier.

Rogers, Everett.
On Diffusion of Innovation.
tstudieninteressierte.uni-hohenheim.de/uploads/tx_uniscripts/25720/A7020_
   KIM_2011.pdf#page=37

Ross, Ralph and Ernest van den Haag. 1957.
The Fabric of Society: An Introduction to the Social Sciences.
New York: Harcourt, Brace.

Sapirstein, Milton. 1955.
The Paradoxes of Everyday Life.
New York: Premier Books.

Saussure, Ferdinand de (trans. W. Baskin). 1915/1966.
Course in General Linguistics.
New York: McGraw-Hill.

Sibley, Mulford Q. 1970.
Political Ideas and Ideologies: A History of Political Thought.
New York: Harper & Row.

Simmel, Georg.
"The Philosophy of Fashion" in Frisby, David and Mike Featherstone (eds.)
Simmel on Culture. 1997.
London: Sage.

Synott, Antony.
"Shame and Glory: A Sociology of Hair," Vol. 38, No. 3, Sept. 1989, 381–413.
British Journal of Sociology.

Theall, Donald F. 2001.
The Virtual Marshall McLuhan.
Montreal and Kingston: Queen's University Press.

Thompson, Michael, Richard Ellis and Aaron Wildavsky. 1990.
Cultural Theory.
Boulder. CO: Westview.

Veblen, Thorstein. 1953.
The Theory of the Leisure Class.
New York: Mentor Books.

Warner, W. Lloyd. 1953.
American Life: Dream and Reality.
Chicago: University of Chicago Press.

Weber, Max (trans. Talcott Parsons). 1958.
The Protestant Ethic and the Spirit of Capitalism.
New York: Charles Scribner's Sons.

Winick, Charles. 1968.
The New People: Desexualization in American Life.
New York: Pegasus.

Winick, Charles. 1995.
Desexualization in American Life.
New Brunswick, NJ: Transaction Books.

Wolfe, Tom. 1970.
Radical Chic & Mau–Mauing the Flak Catchers.
New York: Farrar, Straus and Giraux.

Zeman, J. J.
"Peirce's Theory of Signs" in Sebeok, T. A. (ed.)
A Perfusion of Signs. 1977.
Bloomington: Indiana University Press.

Zukin, Sharon. 2005.
Point of Purchase: How Shopping Changed American Culture.
New York: Routledge.

Index

About the Author

DECODER
MAN

Arthur Asa Berger is Professor Emeritus of Broadcast and Electronic Communication Arts at San Francisco State University, where he taught between 1965 and 2003. He graduated in 1954 from the University of Massachusetts, where he majored in literature and philosophy. He received an MA degree in journalism and creative writing from the University of Iowa in 1956. He was drafted shortly after getting his degree from Iowa and served in the US Army in the Military District of Washington in Washington DC, where he was a feature writer and speech writer in the District's Public Information Office. He also wrote about high school sports for the *Washington Post* on weekend evenings while in the army.

Berger spent a year touring Europe after he got out of the Army and then went to the University of Minnesota, where he received a Ph.D. in American Studies in 1965. He wrote his dissertation on the comic strip *Li'l Abner*. In 1963–64, he had a Fulbright to Italy and taught at the University of Milan. He spent a year as visiting professor at the Annenberg

School for Communication at the University of Southern California in Los Angeles in 1984 and two months in Fall 2007 as visiting professor at the School of Hotel and Tourism at the Hong Kong Polytechnic University. He spent a month lecturing at Jinan University in Guangzhou, China, and ten days lecturing at Tsinghua University in Beijing in Spring 2009.

He is the author of more than one hundred articles published in the United States and abroad, numerous book reviews, and 70 books on the mass media, popular culture, humor, tourism, and everyday life. Among his books are *The Academic Writer's Toolkit: A User's Manual; Media Analysis Technique; Seeing Is Believing: An Introduction to Visual Communication; Ads, Fads And Consumer Culture; The Art of Comedy Writing;* and *Shop 'Til You Drop: Consumer Behavior and American Culture.*

He has also written a number of comic academic mysteries such as *Postmortem for a Postmodernist, Mistake in Identity, The Mass Comm Murders: Five Media Theorists Self-Destruct,* and *Durkheim is Dead: Sherlock Holmes Is Introduced to Sociological Theory.* His books have been translated into German, Italian, Russian, Arabic, Swedish, Korean, Turkish, and Chinese, and he has lectured in more than a dozen countries in the course of his career.

Berger is married, has two children and four grandchildren, and lives in Mill Valley, California. He enjoys travel and dining in ethnic restaurants. He can be reached by e-mail at arthurasaberger@gmail.com.